THE RUSSIANS

HOW THEY LIVE AND WORK

Volumes in the series:

The Russians

HOW THEY LIVE AND WORK

❦❦

W. H. Parker

PRAEGER PUBLISHERS
New York · Washington

BOOKS THAT MATTER

Published in the United States of America in 1973
by Praeger Publishers Inc.
111 Fourth Avenue, New York, N.Y. 10003

Library of Congress Catalog Card Number: 72-93295

Printed in Great Britain

Contents

27809

List of Illustrations

(*The above plates are included by kind permission of Novosti Press Agency except for those acknowledged otherwise*)

Maps

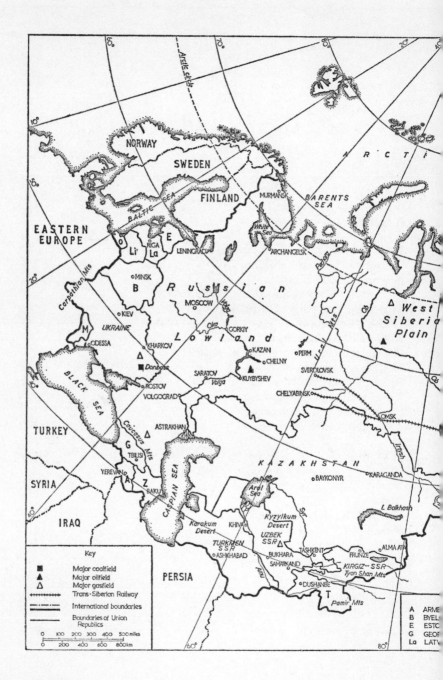

NORWAY

SWEDEN

FINLAND

Arctic circle

BARENTS SEA

MURMANSK

ARCTI

BALTIC SEA

EASTERN EUROPE

o Li'

E

RIGA La

LENINGRAD

White Sea

ARCHANGELSK

West Siberia Plain

△

▲

MINSK

R u s s i a n

B

MOSCOW

o KIEV

UKRAINE

M

ODESSA

△

Donbas

KHARKOV

L o w l a n d

Oka

GORKIY

o

Volga

KAZAN

▲

CHELNY

o PERM

Ural Mts

SVERDLOVSK

o

Carpathian Mts

SARATOV

KUYBYSHEV ▲

Volga

BLACK SEA

o ROSTOV

VOLGOGRAD

CHELYABINSK

OMSK

Irtysh

Ob

TURKEY

Caucasus Mts

ASTRAKHAN

△

G

TBILISI

YEREVAN

SYRIA

A

Z

BAKU

KAZAKHSTAN

Aral Sea

o BAYKONYR

KARAGANDA

o

L. Balkhash

CASPIAN SEA

IRAQ

Karakum Desert

KHIVA

Kyzylkum Desert

Syr

TURKMEN SSR

UZBEK SSR

△

TASHKENT

o

FRUNZE

ALMA ATA

o

IRAQ

PERSIA

o ASHKHABAD

BUKHARA

SAMARKAND

o

Amu

KIRGIZ—SSR

Tyan Shan Mts

o DUSHANBE

T

Pamir Mts

Key

▨   Major coalfield
▲   Major oilfield
△   Major gasfield
++++++++ Trans-Siberian Railway
———— International boundaries
———— Boundaries of Union
        Republics

0   100 200 300 400 500 miles
0   200   400   600   800 km

A   ARME
B   BYEL
E   ESTO
G   GEOR
La   LATV

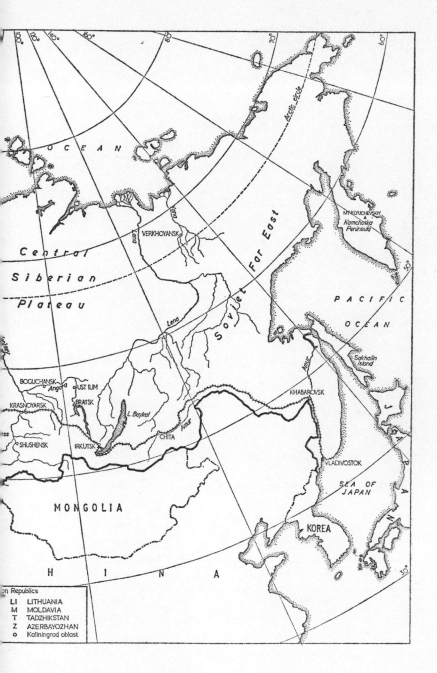

O C E A N

Central

Siberian

Plateau

VERKHOYANSK

Lena

Soviet Far East

MT.KLYUCHEVSKY
Kamchatka
Peninsula

P A C I F I C

O C E A N

Sakhalin
Island

BOGUCHANSK
Angara   UST ILIM
KRASNOYARSK   BRATSK
L Baykal
SHUSHENSK   IRKUTSK   CHITA

KHABAROVSK

J
A
P
A
N

VLADIVOSTOK

SEA OF
JAPAN

MONGOLIA

KOREA

H   I   N   A

on Republics
Li   LITHUANIA
M   MOLDAVIA
T   TADZHIKSTAN
Z   AZERBAYOZHAN
o   Kaliningrad oblast

Introduction

ALTHOUGH often referred to in the West as 'Russia', the great federation which stretches across the Eurasian land mass from the Baltic Sea to the Pacific Ocean, and from the Arctic to the great mountain masses of Central Asia, is formally named the Union of Soviet Socialist Republics or the USSR. Strictly speaking, the name Russia denotes, both historically and geographically, the large area peopled by the East Slavs which extends from the Carpathian Mountains and the plains of Poland in the west to the Ural Mountains in the east. Before the Revolution, the major part of this territory was known as Great Russia, the western borderland as Byelorussia (White Russia), and the south-western lands as Little Russia (now always called the Ukraine). The inhabitants were likewise known as Great Russians, White Russians and Little Russians. Since the Revolution the question of nomenclature has been complicated by the setting up, within the USSR, of the Russian Republic. This not only includes Russia proper (minus Byelorussia, the Ukraine and the Baltic Republics), but reaches across the whole vast extent of Siberia to reach the Pacific.

It is practically impossible to treat 'the Russians' in isolation from the many and varied peoples who also make up the population of the Soviet Union. Even within 'Russia proper', ie west of the Urals, there are many non-Slavic peoples, while beyond the Urals in Siberia, and in the southward extensions of the USSR known as Caucasia and Central Asia, non-Russian peoples predominate. Nevertheless the Russians are by far the largest and most influential national group, and they

11

and their fellow Slavs (Ukrainians and Byelorussians) are alone found well distributed throughout the vast Soviet realm. They are usually the most numerous nationality in the towns, even when the surrounding countryside is non-Slavic in ethnic character, and they tend to hold more than their share of positions of responsibility and power.

Few countries have undergone such a drastic transformation as that which followed the Revolution of 1917 and by which the Russian Empire of the tsars became the USSR. The Revolution not only affected the political organisation of the country but utterly changed the economic and social structure. A new ruling class was fashioned from the Bolshevik revolutionaries, and under their direction the industrialisation of the country proceeded at such a pace that, despite the interruption of the 1941–5 war, the Soviet Union came to occupy a position second only to the United States in industrial output and military strength, while in certain directions of technological advance it took first place. When the fiftieth anniversary of the Revolution was celebrated in 1967, and of the formation of the USSR in 1972, the Soviet form of government seemed to have achieved a stability and durability which had been denied to the English Revolution of the seventeenth century and to the French Revolution of the eighteenth.

The course of history during the years since the Russian Revolution has fully justified the predictions of Sir Halford Mackinder, made in 1904, when he wrote that the great resources of Siberia would one day support a great continental land-based power. In 1919, in his *Democratic Ideals and Reality*, he correctly foresaw that the power of a defeated Germany would rise again under the direction of what he called 'ruthless organisers', that this power would attempt to seize the great riches of the Siberian 'heartland', and that Russia would only survive if she too were regimented by another group of ruthless men into the will and ability to resist the onslaught. He realised that the world as he and his contemporaries knew it, a collection of isolated and disparate continents, would be shrunk by improved communications into an interconnected and interdependent whole in which there would be room for only two great powers. One of these would be based on the Eurasian landmass and would be the victor in a titanic struggle between Russia and Germany for its richly endowed heartland. The other would command the seas and derive its might from maritime trade and influence. He prophesied inevitable rivalry between the great sea power and the great land power, and he warned that unless care was taken, it would be the land-based state, whose might rested upon its control of the heartland, that would prevail in the end. He saw the danger to the maritime world that could develop were the land-based power itself to succeed in its certain strivings to become also a force to be reckoned with at sea.

So it has been, but the simple opposition of two superpowers has now been complicated by the rise of China as a great power and the hostile and threatening stance she has adopted towards the Soviet Union. That China might one day menace Russia's control of the great resources of the Eurasian heartland was also foreseen, in his 1904 paper, by the percipient Mackinder. One effect of this Sino-Soviet split has been for the USSR to seek to improve her relations with Japan and Western countries, and in particular with the United States.

NOTE ON EXCHANGE RATES

When this book went to press the rouble was valued at 47p and at $1.22. At this rate the pound sterling was worth 2.14 roubles, and the dollar 0.82 roubles.

Billion This word has been used throughout the book to indicate a thousand million.

I

The Country and the People

POSITION

THE Soviet Union occupies the northern part of the Eurasian land mass, extending over half way round the globe between latitude 35°N and 78°N, from longitude 19°E of London to 169°W. By far the largest country in the world, its territory amounts to about one-sixth of the land area of the earth. Its area of 8,650,000 square miles is over twice that of the United States and about one hundred times that of the United Kingdom. In shape the USSR roughly resembles an oblong, over twice as long east-west as north-south, with a southward bulge towards the western side. The east-west length varies from a maximum of 5,700 miles to a minimum of 4,600 miles, while the north-south breadth ranges from 2,500 to 1,400 miles. There is a common land frontier with thirteen countries on the western and southern sides, but to the north lies the frozen Arctic Ocean and to the east the Pacific and its associated seas.

GEOGRAPHY

The western part of the country forms the Russian Lowland, which stretches from Poland and the Carpathians on the west to the Ural Mountains on the east, and from the White and Barents Seas on the north to the Black and Caspian Seas on the south, the extent in each direction being about 1,400 miles. Low undulating hills are separated by broad marshy valleys,

14

and although in one or two places the land rises above 1,000ft for the most part it lies between 200 and 600ft. The chief river is the Volga, which, though rising near the Baltic Sea, flows into the Caspian Sea, giving it a length of 2,214 miles. The Volga, like several other rivers of the lowland, notably the Dniester, Dnieper and Don, has a steep high western or right-hand bank and a low, marshy left-hand bank. Between the Black and Caspian Seas, the Russian Lowland terminates in the Caucasus ranges, which include the volcanic Mount Elbruz (18,481ft). The chief range, the Great Caucasus, gives birth to numerous glaciers and fifty descend from the summit of Elbruz alone.

East of the Russian Lowland, beyond the Urals, lies the West Siberian Plain. Except in its southernmost part this is an enormous swamp about 800 miles square. It is the largest extent of flat land on the earth's surface, and except for a few low sandy ridges, this vast ill-drained area lies below 300ft above sea level. It corresponds to the drainage basin of the river Ob (length 3,342 miles). The next region eastwards is the Central Siberian Plateau, which is about 1,000 miles in both length and breadth. This is an upland area with an average height of between 3,000 and 5,000ft, into which numerous streams have cut deep, steep-sided valleys. It is bounded by two great rivers, the Yenisey to the west (length 3,584 miles) and the Lena to the east (length 2,562 miles).

The Central Siberian Plateau is separated from China on the south and from the Pacific Ocean on the east by a broad belt, between 500 and 1,500 miles wide, of high mountain ranges, with several peaks rising above 8,000ft. In the Kamchatka Peninsula the mountains are volcanic: here Mount Klyuchevskiy rises to 15,912ft above sea level, with a crater 300yd wide and 160ft deep. It is one of several active volcanoes and erupted in 1935, 1945 and 1954. Associated with the volcanoes on Kamchatka are many hot springs and geysers. The river Amur (length 1,770 miles) forms the southern boundary of the mountain region for much of its length and also part of the southern frontier of the USSR (with China). But about

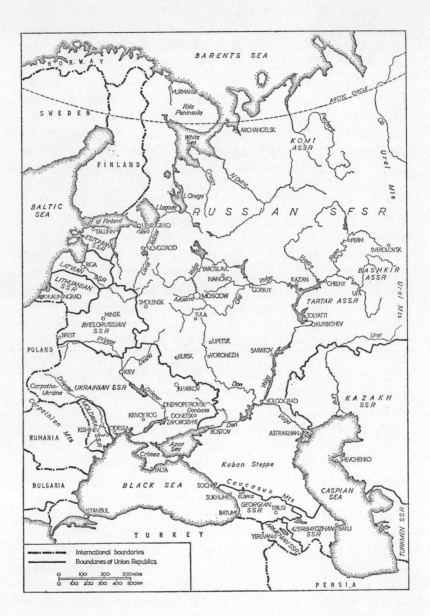

500 miles from its mouth it turns abruptly northwards and flows through the mountains to the Pacific near the northern end of Sakhalin Island.

To the south of the West Siberian Plain and to the east of the Caspian Sea is a large arid area, stretching 1,350 miles from west to east and nearly 1,000 miles from north to south. Here are the great deserts of Soviet Central Asia, some sandy, some rocky and some with surfaces of baked clay. Many of the rivers in this region dry up before reaching any water body, but the two longest, the Amu and Syr, flow into the Aral Sea. They have their origin in the high Pamir and Tyan Shan Mountains, which lie across the south-eastern borders of Soviet Central Asia: here are the highest mountains in the Soviet Union, and some of the highest in the world, notably Mount Communism (24,584ft), Mount Pobeda (24,397ft) and Mount Lenin (23,400ft). Here also is the longest glacier in the world, Fedchenko, a mighty river of ice which flows among the lofty Pamirs.

Besides possessing some of the highest mountains and longest rivers in the world, the USSR has some of the largest lakes. The Caspian Sea (141,480 square miles) is far and away the world's largest lake, while the Aral Sea (23,924 square miles) comes third after North America's Lake Superior (31,500 square miles). Other Soviet lakes of great size are Baykal, Ladoga, Balkhash and Onega, each with an area over 3,500 square miles.

CLIMATE

Almost the whole of the USSR has what is known as a continental climate. This is characterised by severe winters, the severity of which intensifies eastwards: the mean January temperature at Moscow in the west is 14°F (−9·9°C), similar to that of Montreal in Canada or Minneapolis in Minnesota; but at Verkhoyansk in eastern Siberia it is only −59°F (−50·6°C) and the coldest of all the inhabited parts of the earth. Throughout almost the whole of the vast Soviet territory, rivers and lakes freeze and the coasts are fringed with ice for several months.

Spring is the season of the thaw, after which temperatures rise rapidly to give a warm, and in places, a hot summer. The July mean at Moscow is 66°F (19°C), comparable to that of Duluth, Minnesota, but 2° or 3°F warmer than London, England, and even at Siberian Verkhoyansk it is 59°F (15·0°C), which is similar to that of Manchester. But at Odessa on the Black Sea coast it is 72°F (22·4°C)—as high as at Boston, Massachusetts or Nice, while some parts of Soviet Central Asia have July mean temperatures between 73°F (23°C) and 79°F (26°C)—as hot as Washington DC and New Orleans. Autumn is a showery season in which temperatures drop rapidly and rain gives way to snow.

Precipitation comes as snow in winter and as thundery rain in summer in almost every region, but large areas of Soviet Central Asia have very little precipitation at all. The whole country is rather dry. Moscow and Kiev have annual averages of only 21in, while amounts in Siberia are considerably less. Most of the Soviet Union is drier than eastern England, and very much drier than most of the USA. The chief exceptions to these generalisations are to be found along the north-eastern shores of the Black Sea. The Crimean coast, for instance, has an almost typical Mediterranean-type climate: here the famous resort of Yalta is situated. The Black Sea coast near Batumi is the only part of the Soviet Union to have a very large amount of precipitation—nearly a hundred inches in an average year.

The northernmost parts of the USSR have a period of several weeks in winter when there is no daylight and in mid-summer when there is no night.

RESOURCES

Despite its greater size the USSR has less of the resources essential to agriculture—warmth, moisture and rich soils—

than the USA, but its great forests, which extend across the northern part of the country from the Baltic Sea to the Pacific Ocean, give it the world's largest resources of timber, estimated at 2,650 billion cubic feet; these are more than four times those of the United States. The Soviet Union is the only country in the world to be almost completely self-sufficient in mineral wealth, and her reserves of coal, petroleum, natural gas, iron ore and many other metals are greater than America's.

RACIAL ORIGINS

The USSR is a multi-national and multi-racial state. The largest group, the Russians, who make up over half the population, are Slavs, as are the Ukrainians and Byelorussians. There are also about ten million people of European but non-Slavonic origin, principally Lithuanians, Moldavians, Germans, Latvians and Estonians. Nearly one-quarter of the Soviet population is non-European and consists mainly of the Turkic peoples who inhabit Kazakhstan and the Central Asian Republics (Uzbeks, Tartars, Kazakhs, Turkmen, Kirghiz, etc). Although these people are anthropologically distinct from the European population, the difference is not so obvious as that between white and black in America and presents less of an obstacle to racial harmony. Although there is some admixture the numerous races, peoples and nationalities of the USSR remain, on the whole, territorially distinct, each with its own homeland and language.

POPULATION

The population of the USSR at the 1970 census was 242 million. This is a total below that of China and India, but 39 million more than America's and nearly five times that of the United Kingdom. But the Soviet density of population— only 29 per square mile—is much less than that of the USA (58 per square mile) and a mere fraction of that of Britain (over 600 per square mile). If the larger area of the Soviet Union were populated at the same density as the United States, its population would be 600 million.

The birth rate in the USSR has been falling of recent years. This is because there are now fewer potential mothers owing to birth losses in the 1941–5 war. A birth rate of 18·4 per thousand in 1965 had dropped to 17·0 by 1970; meanwhile the death rate has risen slightly to 8·1 per thousand, giving a surplus of births of 8·9 per thousand. These rates are all similar to the American. Infantile mortality has fallen sharply since the war: in 1950 it was 81 per thousand, but in 1970 only 25 per thousand.

State policy is an important factor in Soviet population growth. Since 1936, in order to increase manpower for industrial and military needs, and to make good the heavy wartime loss of life, the Soviet government has pursued a pronatalist policy. Family allowances, maternity benefits, and honours such as the Order of Mother Heroine have been used to stimulate the birth rate. But, owing to an acute shortage of living space in the towns, the artificial limitation of births has, reluctantly, been made possible in the urban areas. Legal abortion was reintroduced in 1955 and contraceptives have become increasingly available.

The Soviet age groups do not diminish regularly from the youngest to the oldest. Various calamities—wars, revolution, civil war, famine, purges—have seriously reduced some of the age groups. Those Russian generations which lived through the most catastrophic periods (1917–25 and 1941–5) are disproportionately short of males. In 1970 there was still a large excess of females in the total population, in which they numbered 130 million or 54 per cent against 111 million males. This excess was confined to the older age groups.

The Soviet people are by no means evenly distributed over the whole territory of the state. Almost three-quarters of them live in a triangular area, with its base along the western frontier and its apex at Irkutsk (near Lake Baykal). This area comprises less than a fifth of the total extent of the USSR. Most of the remaining four-fifths consist of uninhabited or thinly settled tundra, forest, desert or mountainous land. The remaining quarter of the population is crowded into three other, but smaller, zones of concentration: on both sides of the Great Caucasus range and in the irrigated lands of Central Asia.

In 1970 56 per cent of the Soviet population was urban compared with only 48 per cent in 1959, the date of the previous census. The giant multi-million agglomerations in which so much of the American urban population is concentrated are absent. Only Moscow (7,061,000) and Leningrad (3,950,000) have more than 2 million inhabitants, and only eight more towns have over a million. These are Kiev, the Ukrainian capital; Kharkov, a great machine-building and metal-working centre, also in the Ukraine; Gorkiy, an industrial city on the Volga east of Moscow; Kuybyshev, likewise on the Volga, and centre of the great Volga-Ural oilfield; Baku, on the Caspian Sea, capital of the Azerbaydzhan Republic and first city in the world to build its fortunes on the exploitation of an oilfield; Novosibirsk, the west Siberian capital; Tashkent, the capital of Soviet Central Asia; and Sverdlovsk, the metallurgical town founded by Peter the Great in the Urals.

Because the bulk of the population live in high-density blocks of flats, the larger Russian towns are more compact than their Western counterparts, and the relative absence of private motor transport has not permitted large areas of urban sprawl. Most Russian towns in the western part of the country were reduced to rubble during World War II and have been rebuilt with handsome buildings and tree-lined avenues. All Soviet towns are noteworthy for their general tidiness, the absence of hoardings and neon signs, and their regular architecture. Unlike the car-dominated roads of American and European cities, Soviet streets carry mainly buses, trolley buses, taxi-cabs and lorries/trucks, with an occasional donkey cart or hand barrow.

LANGUAGE

Just as there are numerous races, peoples and nationalities in the Soviet Union, so there are very many languages. But wherever Russian is not the native tongue it is taught as the second language, and many non-Russians are bilingual, speaking both their own language and Russian.

Russian is a Slavic language which is made difficult for English-speaking peoples because its root words are usually quite different, and the novice therefore feels himself on more unfamiliar ground than if he were learning French, German or Spanish. Nouns and adjectives have different endings according to their grammatical case and number, and there are further inflexions according to the three genders. Verbs, although possessing a fairly simple tense structure, have two 'aspects', the use of which is extremely difficult to master. As the two aspects are represented by somewhat similar but distinct verb forms, the verb is the chief obstacle to the foreigner's progress in the language. Further difficulty in speaking Russian arises from the stress. For this there is no rule: it may fall on any syllable, and even on different syllables of the same word according to its case or number. The language looks even more formidable than it is because its thirty-six-letter alphabet includes Greek and Hebrew as well as Latin characters. The alphabet does, however, give a fairly reliable guide to the pronunciation. Ukrainian, spoken in the south-west, and Byelorussian, spoken in the western parts, are generally similar to Russian.

Russian is very economical in its use of words. There are no articles; the inflexions of nouns and adjectives and the declensions of the verbs make the use of many prepositions and pronouns unnecessary and the present tense is normally omitted.

NATIONAL CHARACTERISTICS

Those who know the Russians well usually agree that they
are a good-natured, hospitable and, above all, natural and uninhibited people, relatively free of the poses and hypocrisies
that have become commonplace in the West: 'No one who has
remarked the Russian with candour, who judges from what he
sees and not from what he has heard or read, will hesitate to
pronounce him one of the best tempered creatures in the creation . . . A Russian, in the ebullition of passion, may do a
ferocious thing, but never an ill-natured one.' (John Carr,
1804.) It would be a mistake to attribute to the people at large
the ruthless cruelty and indifference to suffering of Ivan the
Terrible, Stalin, his police chief Beria, and other rulers. Neither
Stalin nor Beria was a Russian; both were Georgians. Nevertheless, there does seem evidence that some Russians can be
barbarously cruel, whence perhaps the expression 'Scratch a
Russian and find a Tartar'.

An alternation between extreme gaiety, finding traditional
expression in dance and song, and a morose melancholy, often
accompanied by over-indulgence in alcoholic drink, has also
been noted. Russians seem to combine high animal spirits and
a sense of fun with a remarkable degree of intellectual curiosity.
This is reflected in their passion for the circus on the one hand,
and their love of chess on the other, and since the masses have
learned to read they have become eager buyers of books.

Westerners have always been impressed by the resilience of
the people and their ability to endure all kinds of hardship
and privation without complaint. Richard Chancellor, the
first Englishman to make contact with Muscovy, wrote in the
1550s:

*I believe that they be such men for hard living as are not under the
sun; for no cold will hurt them. Yea and though they lie in the field
two months, at such time as it shall freeze more than a yard thick, the*

common soldier hath neither tent nor anything else over his head: the most defence they have against the weather is a felt, which is set against the wind and the weather, and when snow cometh he doth cast it off, and maketh him a fire and layeth him down thereby . . . Their lying in the field is not so strange as is their hardness: for every man must carry and make provision for himself and his horse for a month or two, which is very wonderful. For he himself shall live upon water and oatmeal mingled together cold and drink water thereto: his horse shall eat green wood and such like baggage, and shall stand open in the cold field without covert . . . I pray you amongst all our boasting warriors how many should we find to endure the field with them one month.

In recent times their endurance has been shown by the herculean labours undertaken on the industrial front in converting the country from a backward peasant state to a foremost industrial nation; by the way in which they sustained the full impact of the German invasion; and by their reconstruction of the national economy, without outside help, within five years of the war's ending. Russians are noted for a sense of humour which is often compared to that of the English. Without it they might well have been less able to endure the trials and tribulations which they have had to bear.

Because of the backward state of the country Russians were once considered stupid, or at best, merely good imitators. This dullness was sometimes attributed to the climate. Only the shrewder observers realised that it was the political and social system of the country that prevented the innate genius of the people from shining forth. Even in the eighteenth and nineteenth centuries, individual Russians were already giving unmistakable signs of remarkable skill and inventiveness. In 1763 the self-taught Polzunov built a steam engine; the contributions of Lomonosov (1712–65) to physics and chemistry were ahead of contemporary European science; and Popov developed wireless communication independently of Marconi.

Thinking Russians have for centuries had a problem of identifying themselves, and there has often been sharp debate between those who have considered themselves as belonging to Europe and the West, and others who have thought of Russia as a world apart with a unique and special destiny for its people. As Dimitri Obolensky has written, 'Most educated Russians have long been conscious of a dichotomy in their cultural inheritance; as early as the beginning of the seventeenth century an acute Russian observer (Ivan Timofeev) remarked: "We are turning our backs to one another; some of us look to the East, others to the West." ' Chinese hostility has of recent years increased the Russian's desire to belong to the European family.

RELIGION

Russia was converted to Christianity in 989, but whereas most European countries received their faith from Rome, the Russians were converted from Constantinople (Byzantium) and adopted the eastern or Greek form of religion. The two branches of the Church parted company in 1054 and became bitterly hostile one to another. When Constantinople succumbed to the Turks in 1453, Moscow assumed its place at the head of the Eastern or Orthodox church; it also inherited the position of leading protagonist against what were considered the errors of the Western way of life as evolved from Roman civilisation under the spiritual guidance of the Catholic Church and its offshoots. Conversion to the Orthodox or Byzantine religion thus set Russia on a different historical path from the West: it meant that she did not experience the various theological, philosophical and intellectual movements which convulsed those countries which had drawn their Christianity from Rome: scholasticism, renaissance, reformation, counter-reformation and enlightenment. The Bolsheviks who came to power in 1917 were the avowed enemies of the Orthodox Church, because in its later history it had been closely associated with the absolutism and autocracy of the tsars. Yet the division between Western capitalism and Eastern socialism, between European individualism and Russian communism, can be traced back to the ecclesiastical schism between Rome and Byzantium.

The Russian Orthodox Church has survived the various vendettas waged against it by the communists, and some churches, attended by mainly older people, remain open, though many others have been closed, or converted into museums or even cinemas. The great mass of the population does not appear to have any religion, although many supposed atheists may have some belief but prefer to keep it private. Persecution of the Church ceased before the war, but the Communist Party still carries on anti-religious propaganda, and anyone with an eye to advancement might think it advisable not to advertise through public worship any faith he might have.

Although most Russians who have any religious belief belong to the Orthodox Church, there appear to have been some Baptist and Jehovah's Witness conversions in recent years. Among the people of the Baltic Republics, and in the western districts of the country which were not inside the Soviet Union until 1940, Roman Catholics and Protestants may also be found. There are also between two or three million Jews in the Soviet Union, many of whom, however, are no longer orthodox. There are only about a hundred synagogues in the USSR, but religious services are often conducted privately in Jewish homes. Although the state permits this it will not tolerate international Zionist activities in the country. In Soviet Central Asia a large proportion of the population still adheres to the Muslim faith.

HISTORICAL LANDMARKS

The Slavs are first heard of in eastern Europe in the first century AD. From the fourth century onwards they expanded in all directions by means of a vigorous colonisation of the territories around them. Those who moved eastwards into the great forests of northern and central Russia are known as the East

Slavs, in contrast to the West Slavs of the Vistula basin (now the Poles) and the South Slavs (or Yugo-Slavs) who penetrated the Balkans. The East Slavs were farmers who made clearings in the forests; they subjugated the more primitive non-agricultural peoples whom they found there, living by hunting.

During the eighth, ninth and tenth centuries the East Slavs fell under the sway of Viking chieftains who entered Russia by river from the Baltic. A geographical peculiarity of central Russia—the region around Moscow, or Muscovy—is that many great rivers, which flow outwards in all directions, have their source in its swampy land. The Vikings soon discovered this and turned it to commercial advantage by using these waterways as trading routes. The most important of these was that which ran from the Gulf of Finland by way of the Neva, Volkhov and Lovat rivers to the great watershed of central Russia, and thence by the Dneiper river south to the Black Sea. This provided a waterway by which the products of northern and southern Europe could be swiftly and profitably exchanged, once the Vikings had made it secure throughout its whole length. These Scandinavian conquerors were known as Russes and they gave their name to the state which they organised.

Under the impetus of river-borne trade, important commercial towns grew up at strategic points on the main routeway from the Baltic to Constantinople, notably Novgorod, Smolensk and Kiev. Kiev, the most southerly of these, enjoying a more genial climate and the support of the more productive lands, became the capital of this early Russia. It was here, towards the end of the tenth century, that Christianity was introduced from Constantinople, a city with which Kiev had developed strong commercial ties. But by this time the Viking bands had been absorbed, through intermarriage and sheer weight of numbers, into one nation—the Russians, Scandinavian perhaps in name, but Slavonic in language and customs. The importance of the fact that the Russians were converted to the Greek rather than to the Roman religion, in setting them apart from other principal nations of Europe, including even their fellow Slavs, the Poles, has already been noted.

From early times the steppes to the south of the great Russian forest had been the home of swift-moving and often ferocious mounted herdsmen. From the beginning their attacks made the southernmost part of Kievan Russia—that section that lay across the steppe—very insecure. In the eleventh and twelfth centuries the nomadic raiders became increasingly dangerous and in 1093 Kiev was sacked. Many Russians fled into the forests and several new towns, including Moscow itself, were founded there. The thirteenth century saw utter disaster. Between 1237 and 1240 a horde of Mongol raiders, the fearsome Tartars of Chingiz Khan, fell upon Russia: they even entered the forest refuges, destroying the towns and subjecting the people to tribute. When a papal envoy to the Tartars arrived at Kiev in 1246 he 'found an innumerable multitude of dead men's skulls and bones lying upon the earth. For it was a very large and populous city, but it was now in a manner brought to nothing.'

The Russians had disappeared from the steppes, except for guerilla bands of survivors who became the Cossacks, equals of the Mongols in horsemanship and ferocity. To the north of the steppes a cowed group of dependent principalities existed in the forests of central Russia, paying tribute to their Tartar overlord. If conversion to the Greek rather than the Roman faith set Russia on a different path from most of Europe, her conquest by the Tartars was a traumatic experience which deepened the difference into a chasm. For while the nations of western and central Europe were growing in wealth and culture, Russia was held down to poverty by the necessity to pay tribute. She succumbed to tyranny because her rulers insisted on absolute mastery over their subjects as a prerequisite for shaking off the Mongol vassalage.

In the sixteenth century an independent Russia once again emerged. But this was not the prosperous Russia of the eleventh, whose cities and churches were a match for any in Europe, but backward and barbarous Muscovy, dominated by a tyrant and isolated in her woods from all contact with the West. All the surrounding peoples were hostile and determined to keep her imprisoned and harmless in her forest dungeon. Ivan the Terrible (1533–84) struggled to set foot on the Baltic but failed. During his reign, however, Muscovy's isolation became a little less acute. In 1553–4 a group of English merchants managed to establish communication with Moscow by way of the Arctic Ocean, and Archangel was established on the shores of the White Sea as Muscovy's first seaport. But if Ivan was not able to fight his way through to the Baltic, his men were now strong enough to deal with the Tartars who blocked his way to the Caspian Sea and Siberia. The Volga lands and Siberia beyond became subject to the Russian tsar and added enormously to his lands, which now constituted a vast empire.

The conquest of Siberia gave the Russians access to a wealth of furs which were greatly in demand in Europe, but no better outlet than northern Archangel, frozen up in winter, was available until the armies of Peter I wrestled the Baltic shore from Sweden at the beginning of the eighteenth century and there built the city of St Petersburg (now Leningrad) at the nearest point on the sea to Moscow. But Russia had to wait until the end of the eighteenth century before victorious wars with the Turks brought her territory once again, after an interval of some six hundred years, to the Black Sea coast. Just as Peter began the building of St Petersburg on the Baltic in 1703 as a new northern outlet, so Catherine the Great in 1794 founded Odessa as the seaport for the wheat-growing steppes of the south. Once again, as in the eleventh century, Russia stretched from the Baltic Sea to the Black, but now she also reached from Poland to the Pacific.

Peter the Great is memorable not only because of his conquests on the Baltic and the foundation of Leningrad, but also for his attempts to westernise Russia. Using the absolute power he had inherited, together with his own abundant energy and brute strength, he attempted to bridge the enormous cultural gap that had developed between Russia and Europe by compelling his people to accept Western teachers and to learn

Western ways. He succeeded in creating a westernised nobility
and court, but did little to change the culture of the mass of
the people, who, sunk miserably into serfdom, looked with
increasing resentment at what had become to them an alien
upper class. In Catherine the Great's reign the gap between a
glittering and luxurious court and a poverty-stricken peasantry
became still wider.

The social structure of Russia in the nineteenth century,
whereby the mass of the population was held in servitude,
arrested economic growth and technological development. The
country again stagnated while its neighbours to the west forged
ahead. This growing gulf between Russia and Europe was
disguised from the world at large for half a century by the
renown the Russians gained from their defeat of Napoleon
(1812). It was not until the Empire's own failures in the Crimean
War (1854–6) that the real weakness of the country was exposed.
As a result various reforms were introduced, including the
liberation of the serfs (1861). But the changes were not radical
enough to avoid further defeat at the hands of Japan in the
Far Eastern war of 1904–5.

In 1905 the country was convulsed with revolution as workers
in the towns and peasants in the countryside rose against their
masters. Feeling humiliated by defeat at the hands of Japan,
Russians of all classes felt the need for change, and the last
tsar, Nicholas II, was forced to concede an elected parliament
or *duma*. It is possible that the old régime might have survived
with the reforms that followed the 1905 disturbances, had not
Russia been involved in war in 1914 and had the imperial
family not fallen under the influence of the monk Rasputin.
The misfortunes of the former and the misgovernment of the
latter destroyed the tsarist state and made it possible for
Lenin's Bolshevik revolutionaries to seize power in 1917.

The twelve years following the Revolution were catastrophic.
Civil war, foreign invasion, famine, intrigue and discord at
the top, chaos, terror and disorganisation throughout, paved
the way for the dictatorship of Stalin, which began in 1929
and lasted till his death in 1953. Stalin, ruthlessly cruel and

resolute, half terrorising and half inspiring the peoples of what was now the Union of Soviet Socialist Republics, achieved the rapid transformation of backward Russia into a highly industrialised state, second in output only to the United States. This timely industrialisation, by creating new industrial areas in the eastern regions, beyond the invader's grasp, made resistance to the German onslaught of 1941 possible and ensured the country's survival. But the damage sustained was appalling: 20 million deaths, the razing to the ground of many towns and thousands of villages, the destruction of whole industrial areas. Although exhausted by the effort and suffering of the war, the survivors had to set to and rebuild their country.

Not till the death of Stalin and the succession to the supreme leadership of the more tolerant and liberal Khrushchev (1954–64) was there some relaxation of the tension and the beginning of a marked improvement in the standard of living. Meanwhile, technological successes, especially in the field of military weapons and space flight, brought increased power to the USSR and enhanced prestige to its leaders.

In recent years the world position of the Soviet Union has greatly changed. From being an outcast and pariah among the nations, her help and friendship are now sought by a growing number of countries, some of them—notably France and Canada—as a counterbalance to the overweening power of the United States, and others, such as India and the Arab states of the Middle East, because they have felt the need of a strong military ally. Against this has to be set the Soviet failure to keep on good terms with the People's Republic of China.

As a result of victory in the 1941–5 war the Soviet Union gained extensive territory in the west, most of which had formed part of the old Russian Empire, but which contained many non-Russians. Beyond her new frontier in eastern Europe, communist governments were established in Poland, East Germany, Czechoslovakia, Rumania, Bulgaria, Hungary, Yugoslavia and Albania. As local communists had played a leading part in resistance movements to the occupying Germans, they had great prestige and weapons in their hands at the end of the war, and the mere proximity of the Russian armies was sufficient to guarantee their successful seizure of power. But as memories of the German atrocities receded and economic difficulties worsened, the communist governments of eastern Europe lost popular support, and in some of them, notably in Hungary in 1956 and Czechoslovakia in 1968, Russian armies have had to intervene to maintain the economic cohesion of COMECON (Council for the Economic Co-operation of the Countries of Eastern Europe) and the military alliance of the Warsaw Pact. Only Yugoslavia and Albania succeeded in leaving the Soviet camp.

A new housing district in Moscow consisting of uniform blocks of apartments, broad tree-lined avenues and lawns.

A worker's family united for Sunday tea. Tea, normally served in glasses in restaurants, etc, is usually drunk from cups in homes nowadays.

2

How the Country Is Run

THE Union of Soviet Socialist Republics came into being on 30 December 1922 as a federation of the Soviet Republics formed in the various parts of the Russian Empire by communist groups after the Revolution of 1917. The Russian Republic, by far the largest and most important, was formed first in 1917, followed by those of the Ukraine, Latvia, Lithuania, Estonia, White Russia (Byelorussia), Georgia, Armenia and Azerbaydzhan. The three Baltic Soviet Republics did not last long, however, but became the independent non-communist states of Latvia, Lithuania and Estonia. The rest became founder Republics of the USSR in 1922. They were joined subsequently by the Uzbek and Turkmen Republics (1925), the Tadzhik

---

This is a new food shop designed to help working women who have little time for shopping. The foods are already partly prepared and can be paid for at the counter. Nevertheless, there are several women waiting. In most shops purchases have to be paid for at a cash desk and a receipt obtained before the goods may be had.

Collective farmers who live within reach of towns may sell produce from their private allotments in markets reserved for the purpose. This is the market at Sukhumi on the Black Sea coast in the Georgian Republic.

Republic (1929) and the Kazakh and Kirghiz Republics in 1936.

In 1940, after the Russians had occupied the Baltic regions, the Soviet Socialist Republics of Lithuania, Latvia and Estonia were revived; Moldavia in the south-west and Karelia in the north-west also became Soviet Republics at about the same time. This made a total of sixteen Union Republics, but Karelia lost this status in 1956, reducing the number to fifteen as it stands at present. Two Republics, Byelorussia and the Ukraine, are members of the United Nations.

The present constitution, promulgated in 1936, but since considerably amended, is a federal one, reserving certain powers to the Union government, others to the Republican governments, while yet others are jointly the responsibility of the Union and of the Republics. The Union government decides questions of war and peace, foreign affairs, security, the armed forces, foreign trade, heavy industry, transport and communications, the monetary system and weights and measures. The Republics are given the power to regulate local government, primary and secondary education, the police, and social and cultural services. Power with regard to agriculture, fisheries, light industry and higher education is shared between the Union and the Republics.

The USSR has a very complex system of administrative divisions. Most of the fifteen Republics are divided into *oblasts* (counties), or *krays* (regions) and autonomous republics: the latter correspond to areas inhabited by nationalities other than that from which the Union Republic takes its name. These autonomous republics have their own governments with certain functions in the social and cultural field. A few *oblasts* and *krays* contain parts distinguished as autonomous *oblasts* and national districts: these again are areas inhabited by a minority people, but one not numerous or advanced enough to have the status of autonomous republic. But in these special areas the administration is carried on in the local language, and national customs and cohesion are preserved.

THE SOVIETS

The government of the USSR is constitutionally a system of elected *soviets*. The word *soviet* means council and refers historically to the workers' councils which were elected in the various factories of Russia in the years preceding the Revolution. At the top is the Supreme Soviet, which is, according to the constitution, 'the highest organ of state power in the USSR'. It is the legislative body: it appoints the Council of Ministers and elects the Supreme Court; it is also responsible for choosing the Presidium—the collective presidency of thirty-seven members whose chairman is head of state. The Supreme Soviet has two 'houses' or 'chambers', the Soviet of the Union, which is elected on a normal constituency basis (one deputy for every 300,000 constituents) and the Soviet of the Nationalities, chosen on a nationality basis, with twenty-five members from each full Republic, eleven from each autonomous republic, five from each autonomous *oblast* and one from each national district. The constituent Republics of the Union and autonomous republics also have their supreme soviets.

Beneath the supreme soviets come various tiers of soviets responsible for local government—first those of the *oblasts, krays* and large cities directly under Republican control; then those for autonomous *oblasts*, national districts, and towns under *oblast* control; below these come the district soviets, and at the bottom of the governmental pyramid are the soviets of hamlets, villages and towns subject to district control.

The meetings of soviets are usually brief and formal. The Supreme Soviet meets for only a few days twice a year, but deputies are expected to remain active in their constituencies throughout the year. Their main work, notably the preparation of legislation and detailed recommendations or criticism of administration, is done by their various standing committees. There are 300,000 of these all told and they play an essential part in the government of the country.

Everyone over eighteen is entitled to vote in the elections for soviets and the ballot is secret. The turn-out at elections is almost 100 per cent, but as there is only one candidate they are mere formalities. The real choice is made by the nominating committees who choose the candidates and over a million people sit on these committees. However, candidates thus nominated can be rejected by the voter who can strike out the name. There is also machinery whereby constituents can recall an unsatisfactory deputy and 498 were so recalled in 1966. Such rejections or recalls occur almost wholly among the local soviets: only ten deputies were recalled from the Supreme Soviet in an eight-year period. Grounds of recall include unworthy conduct such as drunkenness and failure to look after the interests of the constituents and their locality.

THE GOVERNMENT

The government of the Soviet Union is headed by the Council of Ministers. The Ministers are chosen by the Chairman (or Prime Minister) and submitted to the Supreme Soviet for approval. The Council has the executive power to issue orders and decrees within the framework of existing legislation. It also has the right to set aside orders and decrees made by the governments of the Republics. Each minister heads a ministry or government department with headquarters in Moscow and offices throughout the country. These ministries are numerous, for besides the usual ones found elsewhere, such as foreign affairs, labour and public health, there is one for every major industry or sphere of economic activity, eg shipbuilding, ferrous and non-ferrous metallurgy. Some ministries are Union ministries and headed by Union ministers only, while others are Union-Republican ie they are run by representatives both of the Union government and of the governments of the fifteen Republics. Each Republic likewise has its council of ministers, which is responsible to the Republic's own supreme soviet; some of its ministries will be Republican and administer a branch of government wholly within the competence of the Republic, while others will be Union-Republican and associated with the corresponding ministry of the Union Government.

THE COMMUNIST PARTY

On paper, the political system of the USSR, as detailed in the constitution, does not differ very much from that of a Western-style parliamentary democracy. What makes it so different in practice is the fact that the system is worked by a single political party only and that that party is a highly disciplined organisation in which the leadership has a remarkable concentration of power. As a result all the important positions in the higher organs of state are held by those who also occupy prominent places in the Party hierarchy, and this gives the various branches of the Soviet government a remarkable degree of single-mindedness and unity of purpose.

There is but one mention of the Communist Party of the Soviet Union (CPSU) in the constitution, where it is stated that 'the most active and politically conscious citizens from the ranks of the working class, working peasants and working intelligentsia voluntarily unite in the Communist Party of the Soviet Union, which is the vanguard of the workers in their struggle to build a communist society, and is the guiding nucleus of all workers' organisations, public and official.'

The concentration of power within a single party is justified on the grounds that, as there is only one class in the Soviet Union, only one party, that of the working class, is necessary to safeguard its interests. There are over 12 million party members and candidate members, about one in twenty of the population. Their task is to promote the ideals of communism and to foster loyalty to the state, efficiency in administration, productivity in industry, honesty and integrity in socialist enterprises, and a high moral standard of behaviour in all aspects of public and family life. They are expected to be active in all institutions and organisations, whether economic, social, political or administrative. Through them the Party is in everything and is everywhere, advising, supervising, agitating, criticising, encouraging. Through them it counters the inevitable tendency of socialist bureaucracies to be conservative and lethargic, and helps to prevent speculation and corruption. Members are organised mainly by factory, farm or other employing establishment, each of which has its Party committee, but there are also Party organisations corresponding to all the administrative divisions of the country. Every five years or so the membership sends about 5,000 elected delegates to the Party Congress, where the leaders expound the Party's policy and detail its past achievements and future aims.

The Party has a large professional and bureaucratic organisation known as the *apparat* and its members, the Party officials, as *apparatchiki*. Whereas in Western countries lawyers are the group from which most professional politicians are recruited, nearly one half of the Communist Party's officials began their careers as engineers. Successful *apparatchiki* become the leaders of the Party. Those of high rank form the Party's Central Committee. This elects the highest executive body, the Party Presidium or Politburo, but the most powerful body is the Secretariat, which controls all Party appointments. The First Secretaries are the most important men in the Party and therefore in the Soviet Union; this is illustrated by the mere names of the last three to hold the office—Stalin, Khrushchev and Brezhnev. The Central Committee gained considerable authority when Khrushchev appealed to it against a decision of the Presidium to dismiss him, an authority which it was later to use against him—at the time of his downfall in 1964.

The Party devotes much attention to propaganda and agitation, ceaselessly bringing the doctrines of Marx, Engels and Lenin to the attention of the people at large. In doing this it makes use of public meetings, the press, radio and television, wall newspapers, posters and banners, as well as personal persuasion through interviews and conversation with individuals.

The CPSU recruits most of its adult members from the Young

Communist League, a youth movement devoted to fostering the Party's ideals among young people. It has some 23 million members aged between 14 and 28. For children (ages 10–15) the Party organises the Pioneer Corps, which has some resemblance to the Boy Scout movement, and yet younger children, the Octoberites (like Cubs and Brownies).

THE SYSTEM

The Soviet claim that their system is democratic would be regarded as ridiculous by most Westerners. There is little opportunity for political activity or discussion except for that sponsored by the CPSU, and there is no choice of candidates at elections; criticism of the government and its policies may be severely punished as 'anti-Soviet activity'; many of the freedoms guaranteed in the constitution, such as those of speech, of the press, of assembly, and of making processions and demonstrations, exist only for communist and associated organisations. Russia has had a long history of autocracy, bureaucracy and state control, and it is not surprising that its present rulers should employ some of the methods of government used by their tsarist predecessors.

The Soviet claim to be democratic rests upon a different interpretation of democracy from that accepted in the West. It is based on the following facts or suppositions: that the state's interest, rather than the self-interest of individuals and groups, prevails; that the state is made up wholly of workers of one kind or another and that, as the Communist Party is the party of the workers, the workers exercise power through their election of communists to controlling positions in the state; that the state controls the means of production, and that no man may employ another for his own profit; that the one freedom that everyone undeniably has is the right to remunerative work—that there is no unemployment; and finally, that a large proportion of the population participates in the processes of government and administration. There is much truth in this latter claim. There are over 2 million deputies to the 50,000-odd soviets and other governing bodies, and about 60 per cent of these deputies are unpaid amateurs from all walks of life, the remainder being paid professional members of the communist bureaucracy or *apparat*. Associated with the soviets are about 300,000 standing committees on which over 1½ million deputies serve. A large number of citizens work unpaid and part time in numerous organisations such as co-operatives, comrades' courts, street and house committees, parents' associations, pensions committees, volunteer police and fire brigades, etc. Indeed, it has been suggested that as many as 30 million people may be involved, and 'since most of the positions are rotated every few years there can be few Soviet adults who escape the responsibility of direct participation in government' (L. G. Churchward).

The active participation of the ordinary citizen in government is thus far more widespread than in most Western countries. The numerous bodies on which so many people serve not only provide a cheap labour force but help to keep the professional administrators in touch with the needs and feelings of ordinary people; and, because criticism of performance—but not of policy—is encouraged, they provide a check on the efficiency of the official organs of state. No doubt many of these volunteers derive satisfaction from playing a part, however small, in running the country, and the dissidents and malcontents are isolated. Among the latter may be counted many intellectuals and thinking people who cannot admit the claim that all public discussion of policy must be confined within the limits of Marxist-Leninist philosophy as interpreted by the leadership of the CPSU. Also alienated from the system are many individuals who are born 'business men' and whose spirit of enterprise, which might have brought wealth and success in a capitalist country, leads them into prohibited and covert economic activities, such as 'black marketeering' and illegal currency deals.

Some difficulty has also been caused by the growth in the number of undisciplined young people or 'hooligans', but this problem, along with those of violent crime and drug-taking, is on nothing like the scale to be found in Europe or America. More serious, from the Soviet point of view, is a growing awareness among youth of the free and unconstrained way of life permitted to young people in the West, and a desire, the strength of which it is hard to assess, to share in it.

STALIN'S LEGACY

As has happened before in Russian history one man, through the ruthless exercise of unbridled power, has left such a mark upon the country that his influence still persists. Yosif Dzhugashvili, born in 1879 in Georgia, became, under the name of Joseph Stalin, one of the more prominent revolutionaries. As First Secretary of the Communist Party from 1922 he made himself its master, and by unscrupulous use of the secret police, had removed all his rivals by 1929. From now on he was a supreme dictator, stifling all potential opposition by the exercise of a ruthless terror in which hundreds of thousands died and millions were uprooted and sent into exile and to labour camps.

Stalin used his power to transform backward peasant Russia into a powerful industrial state through a series of five-year plans: steelworks, power stations, machine-building factories, canals and railways were built at an astonishing speed. Agriculture was reorganised from individual peasant holdings into collective farms, despite massive opposition. These economic achievements, combined with the heroism of the Russian and other Soviet peoples, made possible successful resistance to, and final triumph over, the Germans in 1941–5. The period until Stalin's death in 1953 saw first the rebuilding of the destroyed towns and industries of Western Russia and then further advances on the economic front; but it also witnessed continued executions and persecutions while the leader himself was deified to an extraordinary degree. These years are now officially referred to as 'the period of the personality cult'.

On Stalin's death the country seemed to heave a sigh of relief, and his successors soon had Beria, Stalin's fellow Georgian and chief of the notorious secret police, shot. From now on violence and murder as a means of securing the position of the top leaders and removing rivals cease, and at the twentieth Party Congress in 1956 Nikita Khrushchev exposed and denounced the excesses of Stalin's reign.

Khrushchev did much to liberalise the system: interference with legal processes was checked; the activities of the secret police were restrained; greater freedom of expression was allowed to writers and artists; and more initiative was encouraged in the lesser organs of government and administration. But the whole system had been corrupted by fear, terror and sycophancy. Too many top posts had been filled in Stalin's time by those who had adapted themselves to such a system and undoubtedly there remain in high places very many 'Stalinists', ie those who believe in the maintenance of absolute power by the Party leadership and the stifling of all criticism and dissent. The liberalising trend initiated by Khrushchev has not been continued; some would say it has been reversed. The present leadership seems to place more weight on raising the material standard of living of the masses, while disregarding the hopes and aspirations of the seeming minority who look for more political and intellectual freedom.

CURRENCY, WEIGHTS AND MEASURES

After the Revolution the *chervonets* was introduced as the monetary unit; it equalled ten of the gold roubles of the former Russian Empire or 7·74234g of fine gold. In 1936 a new gold rouble was introduced and made the monetary unit; its value was linked to the French franc at the rate of 1 rouble = 3 francs. In 1950 the rouble was placed on the gold standard and valued at 0·222168g of fine gold, with 4 roubles equalling 1 US dollar. In 1961 it was up-valued to 0·987412g of pure gold and the official rate of exchange until the 1972 devaluation of the dollar was 1 rouble = $1.11. The rouble is divided into 100 kopeks. It is difficult, however, to arrive at a realistic exchange rate, because some goods in the USSR are very much cheaper than abroad if one applies the official rate, while others are much dearer. A ride on a Soviet bus is only 4 kopeks whereas in an American town it could be 35 cents or more; on the other hand a bar of chocolate costing 25 cents in America might cost a rouble in Russia. Despite the fact that it is a non-convertible currency, the rouble is remarkably stable and has maintained or even increased its purchasing power during the decade since it was revalued in 1961.

Russian money is available in the following notes or bills: 100 roubles, 50 roubles, 25 roubles, 10 roubles, 5 roubles, 3 roubles, 1 rouble; and in the following coins: 1 rouble, 50 kopeks, 20 kopeks, 15 kopeks, 10 kopeks, 5 kopeks, 3 kopeks, 2 kopeks and 1 kopek. Denominations of 10k and above are 'silver', of 5 and below, 'copper'.

The metric system was adopted in 1927 but some of the old Russian measures continue in popular use and are met with in literature. The commonest are the *verst* (about two-thirds of a mile), the *arshin* (28in), the *desyatin* (2·7 acres approx), the *pud* (36lb) and the *chetvert* (5·77 bushels approx).

TAXATION

Personal taxation in the USSR during the late 1960s amounted to 50 billion roubles or about 40 per cent of personal incomes, but real income is rising faster than taxation. Taxes are mainly indirect, over 80 per cent coming from a turnover tax. Thus the Russian pays his taxes when he buys goods and services. Direct taxation has been progressively reduced.

POLICE

The police force or militia is under local control and performs similar functions to police forces elsewhere. It is aided by a 3 million strong organisation of civilian volunteers known as *druzhinniki*: these are so numerous and widespread throughout the community, though unobtrusive because of their civilian dress, that they are often able to deal with trouble without recourse to the regular police. The special or secret police, of whom so much is heard, are concerned with matters of security, and the ordinary visitor to the Soviet Union is no more likely to come across them than is the average Soviet citizen. If, however, he should visit or meet Soviet citizens who are themselves under suspicion, then he might make their acquaintance.

JUSTICE

Under Khrushchev (1954–64) serious attempts were made to restore the rule of law and to bring the actions of the security authorities and the secret police under control. Measures were taken to protect persons charged with grave offences, and the security authorities were forbidden to punish without trial; procedures were established for the inspection of labour camps and prisons; deportation, banishment and deprivation of citizenship were abolished; secret trials were ended, and the obligation to prove guilt placed on the prosecution; legal representation was made available for all defendants.

Soviet courts are remarkably democratic. The lower courts (people's courts) consist of a judge, elected for five years, and two lay assessors, elected for two years. Elected assessors also sit on the higher courts. Assessors serve for two weeks in the year. The people's courts deal with all minor offences, civil and criminal, and there is the right of appeal from them to the *oblast* courts, which also try more serious cases. The most important cases come before the supreme courts of the Republics or autonomous republics, while the most important issues of all are dealt with by the Supreme Court of the USSR. The various Republican and local authorities can make their own rules and regulations for the administration of justice within the general framework of the Union laws. The language of the predominant local nationality is used in the courts, and interpreters are made available where the plaintiffs or defendants have a different language.

Sentences for serious crimes usually include a spell in a labour camp. Capital punishment was abolished in 1947, but was brought back in 1950 for serious offences against the state, and in 1954 for certain kinds of murder.

THE ARMED FORCES

Soon after the Revolution of 1917, the Bolsheviks found that they would need regular armed forces if they were to survive the counter-revolutionary operations of the White armies and foreign military intervention. Consequently, on 15 January 1918 the Council of People's Commissars resolved that 'a new army, the Workers' and Peasants' Red Army, shall be formed'. At first it was to be a volunteer force, and the decree stated that it would 'be built up from the most class-conscious and organised elements of the working classes' and that 'everyone who is ready to give his energies and his life to defend the gains of the October Revolution, Soviet power and socialism joins the Red Army'. However, as Russia had been fully involved in the war with Germany for over three years and people were tired of fighting, a voluntary force was not enough and in April 1918 universal conscription was introduced.

The army so raised defeated the White armies in the Civil War of 1918–20 despite the support given to the latter by Britain, France, the United States, Italy and several other Western states. Political ideology was stressed from the beginning, and a catechism was devised to ensure that Red Army men knew what they were fighting for. This began as follows:

Q. What are you, comrade?
A. I am a defender of all working people.
Q. What are you fighting for?
A. For justice, so that the land, the factories, the rivers, the forests and all riches belong to the working people.
Q. What are you fighting with?
A. I am fighting with rifle, bayonet and machine gun, and

also with the word of truth addressed to the enemy's soldiers, to his workers and peasants, so that they should know I am their brother and not their enemy.

The communists have never ceased to indoctrinate the armed forces, which are carefully watched by political commissars attached to all units. In this way the Party has maintained its supremacy and prevented the threat of military dictatorship. Tight Party control enabled Stalin to remove and execute a large number of the leading officers during the great purges of 1936–8. It made it possible for the Party to remain in control during the desperate years of the 1941–5 war with Germany, when the country was so utterly dependent upon the armed forces. And it gave Khrushchev the assurance that he could remove the popular war hero, Marshal Zhukov, in 1957, when that famous soldier appeared to chafe under the Party's supervision.

The liquidation of so many of the Red Army's experienced senior commanders and officers by Stalin was doubtless responsible for much of the confusion and defeat that followed the German invasion of 1941. On the other hand, the rapid promotion of the more able junior officers which followed probably, in the long run, contributed to success. Since the great victories of 1945 the Red Army has not had to fight a major battle, although its power has been used to prevent threats to the stability of some of the communist governments in eastern Europe. In fact, the Red Army—now the Soviet Army—is today more widely known for its cultural activities, for one tradition of tsarist Russia that has continued into modern times is that of the educated and accomplished army officer. The Soviet Army Ensemble is famous for its singing, dancing and musical performances. The army also has its own theatre where classical dramas —including Shakespeare—are acted with outstanding talent.

The Soviet Navy is of much more recent growth but is now in process of rapid expansion. At the time of the 1941–5 war there were only 3 old battleships dating from before the Revolution, and 5 cruisers, only 2 of which were recent. After the the war a modern navy was created, which is now second only to that of the United States. Surface vessels include 18 cruisers and 48 destroyers equipped with surface-to-surface or surface-to-air missiles, as well as numerous other ships: escorts, patrol boats, mine sweepers and landing craft. The submarine fleet, which consists of about 290 conventionally powered and 80 nuclear-powered vessels, is especially formidable. Fifty-six submarines are equipped to fire ballistic missiles. Unlike the American navy, the Soviet fleet does not include aircraft carriers, although it has 2 helicopter carriers. The total strength is about 475,000 men.

It is not generally realised to what extent Russia participated in air warfare during the 1914–17 conflict. The first bomber squadron was formed in 1915 and Murmets machines raided targets in East Prussia. Immediately after the Revolution a Soviet air detachment was formed, and in the 1920s Tupolev was designing heavy bombers comparable to any in the West— the TB-1s and TB-3s. When war came in 1941 the Soviet Union was well prepared in the air and possessed over 3,000 combat aircraft. This strength in the air was a vital factor in Russia's survival of the first critical months of the German invasion. The total strength of the Soviet Air Force today is about 480,000 men and it has over 10,200 combat aircraft. The long-range bomber force is relatively small compared with the American, but the tactical air force, designed to support the army in the field, is very strong—over 4,000 aircraft, including light bombers, ground attack and interceptor-fighters, helicopters, transport and reconnaissance planes. That part of the air strength known as the naval air force is, in fact, land based, but located near the shores of the White, Baltic and Black Seas, and capable of ranging over those waters in concert with the navy.

In strategic military weapons the Soviet Union has near parity with the United States. Each superpower had well over 2,000 warheads in 1970, but the type of delivery system varied in importance. Most Soviet warheads—1,300—were mounted on land-based intercontinental ballistic missiles whereas the majority of America's were on sea-launched ballistic missiles (1,328), although the United States also had 1,074 ICBM warheads. Besides her 1,300 ICBM warheads, Russia had 700 on intermediate-range and medium-range ballistic missiles.

Just as most western European powers associated with the United States are organised in NATO, so most of the eastern European countries are linked with the Soviet Union in the Warsaw Pact, which includes the USSR, Bulgaria, Czechoslovakia, East Germany, Hungary, Poland and Rumania. And just as the top posts in NATO are held by Americans, so the Commander-in-Chief of the Joint High Command of the Warsaw Pact has always been a Soviet officer. None of the Pact members, other than the Soviet Union, has nuclear weapons at its disposal.

In 1970 military expenditure by the Soviet Union was an estimated $40 million compared with $74 million by the United States. There are many difficulties in the way of assessing the real Soviet outlay in terms of US dollars, but it is generally accepted that the American military budget is much larger. This is only to be expected, since America has commitments ranging over all the continents of the globe. Also the firms working on military contracts for the US government expect to make profits, and most expenses—notably the pay of an American soldier—are much higher than the cost of equivalent items in the USSR.

The problems created by housing the population in large high-density apartment blocks are met to some extent by the space afforded by broad tree-lined avenues. Here, in the Siberian town of Akademgorodok, young mothers meet and children play.

Some state farms in the Soviet Union are of immense size and the tractor teams often have to camp in semi-permanent hutments away from home. Here such a camp, in the vast steppe of southern Siberia, is visited by a mobile shop.

3

The Republics and the Regions

ALTHOUGH the Soviet Union is a federation of fifteen Republics, it is also divided for certain administrative and statistical purposes into economic regions, of which there are nineteen. Ten are in the Russian Republic and three in the Ukrainian Republic. The Kazakh, Byelorussian and Moldavian Republics are also economic regions, while the Baltic, Trans-caucasian and Central Asian Republics form three more such regions. The boundaries of the regions never cross those of the Republics or of *oblasts*.

The Russian Socialist Federative Soviet Republic, with an area of $6\frac{1}{2}$ million square miles, is nearly twice the size of the USA and over seventy times as large as the UK. It is by far

---

The dry steppes of southern Siberia and northern Kazakhstan were ploughed up for the first time in the 1950s. Yields have varied greatly owing to the unreliable rainfall, but in most years millions of tons of wheat are harvested. The crop is brought to a threshing centre such as this and then taken to the rail station by lorry/truck.

Almost daily new mineral finds are made in the vast territory of the USSR. Here a drilling party, supervised by a geologist, is prospecting for gold in the Chita district of eastern Siberia.

the largest of the fifteen Union Republics, and possesses three-quarters of the area of the USSR. In population it is less dominant, but still holds well over half (54 per cent) of the total. Of its 130 million inhabitants 108 million, or 83 per cent, are Russians, the remainder being divided among numerous ethnic groups, most of which have their identity recognised in the organisation of their homelands as autonomous republics and national districts.

Because of the length of its full name, the Republic is normally referred to either as the RSFSR or as the Russian Federation. Its capital is Moscow.

RUSSIA

That part of the Russian Federation lying to the west of the Urals is Russia proper, as distinct from Siberia to the east. Although only one-fifth of the area of the whole Republic, Russia contains 90 million inhabitants, or almost 70 per cent of the population.

Geographically Russia is a vast lowland which extends for 1,500 miles from the White Sea in the north to the Sea of Azov and the Caucasus Mountains in the south. Hills and morainic ridges which cross the north-central part of the lowland from west to east act as a great divide between northward-flowing streams such as the Volkhov, Onega, Dvina and Pechora, and longer southward-flowing rivers, notably the Don and the Volga. The north-western area abounds in lakes, torrents and waterfalls. Distinctive landscapes, based on dominant vegetation types, cross the country in broad zones from north to south. Along the shores of the Arctic Ocean there is the stony treeless tundra, snow- and ice-covered throughout the long dark winter, but noisy with birds and gay with tiny flowering plants during the brief summer thaw. South of the tundra is a broad belt of *tayga* forest in which the coniferous spruce is predominant, but there are also many pine and birch trees. Mixed forest, in which oak and other broad-leaved trees appear alongside the spruce, birch and pine, predominates in the land between the upper

Volga and its tributary the Oka. This area is the ancient Muscovy or Moscow region, and it was here that the Russian nation was reborn after the Mongol conquest of the thirteenth century. South of the Oka the forest begins to diminish and expanses of open country appear; and eventually the woodland disappears entirely, except in river valleys, to make way for true steppe. This, before it was ploughed up, covered the lands bordering the Sea of Azov and those lying north of the Caucasus Mountains.

Russia proper is divided into six economic regions. One of these, the Central Industrial or Moscow region, is the foremost industrial area of the Soviet Union, with important metalworking, machine-building, chemical and textile industries. Over 7 million of this region's population of 28 million are in Moscow, the three next largest towns being ancient Yaroslavl (population 520,000) on the Volga, the steel-making town of Tula (470,000), and a cotton-manufacturing creation of the nineteenth century—Ivanovo (420,000).

Moscow emerged in the twelfth century as a fortress town on a defensible site in the watershed area of the mixed forests of central Russia. With waterway routes radiating in all directions it not only became a great trading centre but was chosen as the most suitable place from which to administer the surrounding lands. As the Muscovite state expanded so the importance of Moscow grew, and the Russian Orthodox Church made it an ecclesiastical capital as well. In 1712 it lost its status as seat of government to St Petersburg (Leningrad), and was burned down in 1812 at the time of Napoleon's invasion of Russia; but the second half of the nineteenth century saw the rapid industrialisation of the city, and its population rose from 462,000 in 1863 to over 1 million in 1897. In 1918 it became capital once more.

Moscow has been transformed during the Soviet period into a great modern capital with broad tree-lined avenues, and tall blocks of administrative buildings and flats, but the historic centre has been preserved. Here Red Square, with the ornate St Basil's Cathedral, and the squat Lenin mausoleum, stands between the Kremlin on the one side and the State Universal

Stores (GUM) on the other. The Kremlin was the prince's stronghold and encloses palaces, churches and gardens. GUM consists of whole arcades of shops within an immense three-storey building, built on the site of the great market which, since medieval times, assembled here a wide variety of goods from many parts of the world.

The economic region of the North-West contains Leningrad, the second largest city of the USSR with a population of nearly 4 million. Peter the Great founded the town in 1703 as a seaport and naval base at the point on the Baltic coast nearest to Moscow. He made it capital of the Russian Empire in 1712, a position it held for two centuries, and during that period it was adorned with many splendid buildings. It lies, however, as far north as the sixtieth parallel, and has been described as 'majestic, spacious, even beautiful, cold, sunless, tragic, mysterious, dank and gloomy, like the forests that surround it' (Nevill Forbes, 1918). It was known by the German name of Petersburg until the outbreak of war with Germany in 1914, when the name was translated into Russian as Petrograd. After the death of Lenin in 1924 it was renamed Leningrad. The city suffered severe hardships during the siege by the Germans in the 1941–5 war and over a million of its citizens died from hunger, disease and enemy bombardment. Leningrad is a very important industrial centre and at its famous Electrosila works were made the generators for the great hydro-electric stations of Siberia as well as those for Egypt's Aswan dam. The region reaches up to the White Sea, on the shores of which the port of Archangel (population 350,000) was founded in the reign of Ivan the Terrible (1533–84) for trade with England and Holland, and also to the Barents Sea coast, where the fishing centre of Murmansk sustains a population of 310,000 well within the Arctic Circle.

The Volga-Vyatka region lies to the east of the Central Industrial region and contains the great machine-building city of Gorkiy (population 1,200,000), which, as Nizhniy Novgorod, was famous before the Revolution on account of the great trading fair held there annually. Southwards from it the Volga economic region extends along the great river to the Caspian

Sea. It is noteworthy for its great oil and gas fields, which lie mostly in the Bashkir autonomous republic, and for the large hydro-electric stations built on the Volga. Its leading towns are all on the great river, and are, from north to south, Kazan (population 990,000), capital of the Tartar autonomous republic; Kuybyshev (1,050,000), the oilfield capital; Saratov (760,000), an important bridge town; Volgograd (820,000), the former Stalingrad and site of the decisive battle of the 1941-5 war; and Astrakhan (420,000), the old Tartar port of the Volga delta and centre of the caviar industry.

The two remaining Russian economic regions, the Central Black Earth and the North Caucasus, are both predominantly agricultural, having been blessed with the richest soil in the country—the fertile black earth or *chernozem*. To the resources of the Central Black Earth region, which lies immediately to the south of the Central Industrial region, must now be added the immense reserves of iron ore near Kursk, which began to be worked in the 1960s. Voronezh (population 670,000), which is the largest town of the region, has a big nuclear power station in its vicinity. The great plains of the North Caucasus region, which lies north of the Caucasus Mountains, are famous for their high wheat yields and their colourful Don Cossacks, but this region now has a valuable mineral resource in the form of prolific gasfields. Its capital is the industrial town and port of Rostov (population 900,000) near the mouth of the river Don.

THE URALS

The Ural chain is a remarkably straight line of mountains and hills which closely follow the sixtieth meridian E and divide Russia from Siberia. In early times they were regarded by the Russians as the limits of their known world, and were not crossed in any strength until late in the sixteenth century. Their central area, which forms the Ural economic region, has the widest range of mineral wealth of any comparable area in the world, and this fact has led to its industrialisation. This region, with only 3 per cent of the area of the Soviet Union, now produces 31 per cent of its steel, 21 per cent of its paper, 19 per cent of its oil, 15 per cent of its electricity and 14 per cent of its machine tools. Its population of 15 million is mostly urban, owing to the restricted agricultural possibilities of a cool and hilly region, and inhabits such large industrial centres as Sverdlovsk (population 1,026,000), Chelyabinsk (874,000) and Perm (850,000).

SIBERIA AND THE FAR EAST

Over 25 million people live in that vast territory of the RSFSR which extends eastwards from the Urals to the distant Pacific. Mostly they inhabit a narrow zone which follows the Trans-Siberian Railway (TSR) and which is hemmed by cold forested country to the north and by mountains to the south. There are only three economic regions, each of immense size: West Siberia, East Siberia and the Far East.

The West Siberian region includes in its southern part much good agricultural land and the important Kuzbass (Kuznetsk basin) coalfield, with an annual production of well over 100 million tons of coal, some of which is used in local steelworks. Where the railway crosses the great northward flowing Siberian rivers large industrialised towns have grown up, notably Novosibirsk (TSR and river Ob, population 1,170,000) and Omsk (TSR and river Irtysh, 830,000). But the central and northern parts of the region are a vast swamp: the flat land, with its subsoil permanently frozen, is unable to drain away the water brought from the mountains to the south by the Ob and its tributaries. It is planned to divert some of this surplus water southwards to the arid lands of Central Asia. During the 1960s great oil and gas deposits were discovered beneath the marshy lands of the central and northern parts of West Siberia, and these fields are becoming increasingly productive, despite the appalling working conditions caused by the extremely low winter temperatures, and by the mud and mosquitoes of this ill-drained land in summer.

In the East Siberian region the narrow belt of population, farming and industrialisation comes close to the mountainous southern border of the country, while northwards to the Arctic there are vast expanses of forested hills and plateaus and treeless tundra. Winter temperatures are among the lowest on the earth's surface, but summers are often quite warm. Two great rivers, the Yenisey and the Lena, flow across the region from south to north, and where the Yenisey and its tributary, the Angara, flow through deep, steep-sided valleys, some of the largest hydro-electric stations in the world have been built or are under construction. These are at Shushensk (ultimate installed capacity, 6·4 million kW), Krasnoyarsk (6·0 million kW), Bratsk (4·6 million kW), Ust Ilim (4·5 million kW) and Boguchansk (4·0 million kW). The largest hydro-electric stations in the USA are Grand Coulee and John Day, both on the Columbia river, with ultimate capacities designed to be 5·5 million and 2·7 million kW respectively. Throughout East Siberia there are rich and varied mineral resources, but many of the sites are difficult of access and the severe winter temperatures and permanently frozen ground present acute problems. The chief cities of East Siberia are Krasnoyarsk (population 660,000), where the TSR crosses the Yenisey river, and Irkutsk (460,000), where it crosses the Angara.

In the Far East population is again forced by the hostile environmental conditions of the immense tracts to the north to keep close to the southern frontier of the USSR. Here the seaport and naval base of Vladivostok (population 450,000), Pacific terminus of the TSR and the inland industrial centre of Khabarovsk (440,000), built where the TSR crosses the great Amur river, are the chief urban centres. Negotiations at present being conducted with the Japanese could lead to their cooperating with the Soviets in developing the immense forest and mineral resources of the Far East. Such a development would solve Japan's raw material supply problems, and as China lays claim to much of the Soviet Far East, the Soviet Union would welcome some Japanese involvement.

Since its conquest in the sixteenth century, Siberia has been used by successive governments as a place of exile, and many of the inhabitants are descended from those who were banished into its hostile environment. The industrialisation of many areas in the south—and of the Urals—during Stalin's first five-year plans enabled the Soviet Union to survive the 1941–5 war, for after the old-established western industrial areas had been lost, supplies of material continued to flow from the new factories of the east. Siberian troops, renowned for their ferocity, played a leading part in the salvation of Moscow during the critical winter of 1941–2.

THE UKRAINIAN AND MOLDAVIAN REPUBLICS

These two Republics, which lie east of the Carpathian Mountains and north of the Black Sea, make up less than 3 per cent of the area of the USSR (Ukraine, 2·7 per cent; Moldavia 0·2 per cent), but they contain 21 per cent of its population. Most of the inhabitants of the Ukraine are Ukrainians (36 million out of 48 million) but there are also nearly 10 million Russians and sizeable minorities of Jews, Byelorussians and Moldavians. The Ukraine is about the size of France in both area and population.

The Ukrainians were formerly called 'Little Russians' by the Russians, not because they are smaller physically—if anything, the reverse is the case—but because their country, smaller in size, was known as Little Russia. They are a distinct nation with their own language, although this is Slavonic and differs only slightly from Russian. They regard the Russians much as the Bavarians regard the Prussians, and possibly as the Irish regard the English. They have had their own history, which ran a different course from that of the Muscovites. They are proud of the fact that the early Russian state which flourished in the eleventh and twelfth centuries, and was then the equal of any European country in civilisation and commerce, was centred on the Ukraine and had its capital at Kiev. But this early Russia lay too exposed to raids by the ferocious nomadic horsemen of the steppe, who came in waves out of the east. It was these incursions that split the Russians into Muscovites and Ukrainians. Bands of refugees made their way either into the forests of the north-east (Muscovites), or into Poland and the Carpathian country to the west (Ukrainians). And whereas the Muscovites, isolated in their forest fastnesses, were cut off from cultural contact with Europe for centuries, the Ukrainians lived in close contact with the Poles and other western peoples, and were in many ways influenced by them.

From the thirteenth to the sixteenth centuries most Ukrainians lived under Polish and Lithuanian rule, but independent bands of Cossacks continued to defy Pole, Turk and Tartar alike. From the fifteenth century on Muscovy, in a succession of wars, began to win back Ukrainian territory from the Poles, and at the same time her frontier was pushed southwards from the forest towards the steppe. Much of this land, newly won from the Turks, was colonised by Ukrainians from the Polish-held lands west of the Dnieper river. By the end of the eighteenth century most of the Ukraine lay within the borders of the Russian Empire, and although its people had originally welcomed freedom from Polish rule and union with people of similar language, religion and race, they soon discovered that the autocratic rule of the Russian tsars was no less oppressive than that of the Polish nobility, and the peasants, like those of Russia, were reduced to serfdom. The tsars attempted the russification of the Ukraine and strove to suppress all manifestations of a distinct Ukrainian nationality. This aroused strong anti-Russian emotions and led to the formation of an independent republic of the Ukraine in 1917, after the Russian Empire had collapsed into anarchy. This was recognised by the Germans in March of 1918, but in 1919 Ukrainian communists set up a rival government which eventually prevailed, and the Ukraine became one of the constituent republics of the USSR in 1922.

The modern history of the Ukraine has been a tragic one. Disaster followed disaster. Millions died of starvation in the famines of the 1920s and during the disruption caused by Stalin's forced collectivisation of agriculture during the late 1920s and early 1930s. Hundreds of thousands more disappeared into labour camps in remote parts of the Soviet Union. In 1941 the Nazi armies entered the Ukraine. Any hope that the Germans might again encourage the formation of an independent Ukraine soon vanished: they behaved as harsh conquerors, and Ukrainians united with Russians in resisting the invaders. But the country was devastated, not only by the fighting, but by the scorched-earth policy of the retreating Russians. While the Soviets evacuated large numbers of the population eastwards to the Urals and West Siberia, equally large numbers were carried off to Germany to work in war factories there. The Russian advance of 1943–4 and the German retreat brought another wave of devastation, and in the immediate postwar period Stalin's inquisition hunted out alleged collaborators and shot or exiled them. The only advantage the 1941–5 war brought to the Ukraine was its territorial enlargement by the acquisition of Bessarabia and North Bucovina from Rumania and of the Carpatho-Ukraine from Czechoslovakia. These had been part of old Kievan Russia before the Mongol conquest and were still largely peopled by Ukrainians.

The Ukraine is divided into three economic regions. One of these, the Donets-Dneiper region, is heavily industrialised. Possessing in the Donbass (Donets basin) a foremost coalfield, and at Krivoy Rog the most productive iron ore field in the world, along with large reserves of manganese, salt and natural gas, it has developed metallurgical, engineering and chemical industries on a large scale. These industries are found chiefly in and around the great cities of Kharkov (population 1,250,000), Donetsk (880,000), Dnepropetrovsk (870,000) and Zaporozhye (670,000). The village of Donetsk was renamed Yuzovka after a British iron manufacturer, Hughes, who established an iron-works there in the 1870s. In 1935, greatly enlarged by industrial expansion under the first five-year plan, it was renamed Stalino. It is now once more Donetsk and the central city of a great coalfield conurbation numbering some five million inhabitants.

The South-West economic region is made up mostly of rich black earth agricultural land, but it also includes, in the extreme west, a section of the Carpathian Mountains, with valuable forest and mineral resources. In this region is the historic capital of the Ukraine, Kiev (population 1,700,000). The town began as a fortified settlement on the high right-hand bank of the Dnieper, and after ancient Russia's conversion to the eastern form of Christianity in 989, became a city of churches built in the Byzantine style. This large, rich and populous city experienced increasing difficulty in defending itself against nomadic horsemen and in 1239 it was totally destroyed by the Tartars. After a long period of Lithuanian or Polish rule it was won back by the Muscovites in 1654, but it remained little more than a garrisoned frontier outpost until the late eighteenth century. Most of Poland was then incorporated in the Russian Empire and Kiev ceased to be an exposed border town. During the nineteenth century it grew rapidly to become a large industrial and commercial centre. In September 1941, almost seven centuries after its sack by the Mongols, it was taken by the Germans and again suffered extensively. It has been rebuilt with spacious tree-lined avenues: older buildings have been reconstructed in Ukrainian baroque while many grand new edifices have been erected in neo-classical and Soviet styles.

The third economic region of the Ukraine is the South, made up of the wheat-growing steppe lands bordering the Black Sea and including the Crimean Peninsula. Mountains skirt the southern shores of the Crimea and drop picturesquely to the sea and there are resorts and bathing beaches along the coast. The largest town of the region is the seaport of Odessa (population 900,000), founded in 1794 by Catherine the Great to provide an outlet for the wheat from the fertile steppe which she had just won from the Turks. The small Moldavian Republic specialises in fruit growing. The capital, Kishinev, had a population of 357,000 in the 1970 census.

THE BALTIC REPUBLICS

The three Republics of Lithuania, Latvia and Estonia, which border upon the Baltic Sea, have a combined area of 75,000 square miles—somewhat smaller than Great Britain and roughly the size of the State of Nebraska. They contain some 7 million inhabitants, mainly Lithuanians (2,507,000 at the 1970 census), Latvians or Letts (1,342,000), Russians (1,308,000) and Estonians (925,000). The three Baltic nations have a long history of foreign domination, whether by Poles, Swedes, Germans or Russians, but they experienced a brief interlude as nominally independent sovereign states from 1918 to 1940. Previously they had formed part of the Russian Empire; now they are constituent Republics of the USSR. Lying between the great warrior nations which have for centuries fought to control the Baltic, these Baltic lands have been repeatedly devastated by war. Along with Kaliningrad *oblast*, they form the Baltic economic region. Kaliningrad *oblast* consists of part of the former German province of East Prussia.

The Baltic region is a lowland diversified by hummocky hills, undulating plains and badly drained depressions. Marshes and small lakes are common amidst the morainic hills, which are ridges and mounds of clay, sands, gravels and boulders gathered up by the great ice sheets of the Ice Age on their advance and dropped haphazardly as they melted away. About a third of the area is covered by forest. There are some favoured areas with better drainage and soils where cereals and sugar beet are grown or where market gardens work to supply the cities with vegetables, but the predominant form of agriculture is livestock rearing with some flax and potatoes. There is little mineral wealth apart from the Estonian oil shales, which are exploited for the generation of electricity and the manufacture of chemicals. Centrally placed Riga (population 750,000) is the capital of the Baltic region and of the Latvian Republic. It is a great seaport and manufacturing town and, like the other large cities of the region, preserves medieval quarters with narrow crooked streets and old German architecture, to which have been added new blocks of flats and factory buildings.

THE BYELORUSSIAN REPUBLIC

This Republic has an area of 88,000 square miles, making it comparable to Great Britain and slightly larger than Minnesota, and the 1970 census gave it a population of 9 million. Most of these (over 7 million) are Byelorussians (White Russians), who like the Ukrainians, became differentiated from the Muscovites or Great Russians after the Mongol conquest of the thirteenth century. They speak a language very similar to Russian. There are also nearly a million Russians and 383,000 Poles. The Republic is an economic region of the USSR.

Byelorussia formed part of Lithuania or Poland until the late eighteenth century when it was incorporated into the Russian Empire by Catherine the Great. Much of it was again held by Poland between 1919 and 1939. It was mercilessly ravaged during the 1941–5 war. Apart from some morainic ridges, it is a flattish land with poor soils and much forest and swamp. The better-drained parts produce rye, while hemp and flax are also grown; elsewhere livestock and potatoes are characteristic of the farming. Because of wartime destruction most farm buildings are new, but many of the old log houses, re-roofed with asbestos, remain. Much of the countryside has a poverty-stricken appearance and women and horses are still found at work as well as modern farm machinery. There are few minerals, but the discovery in 1972 of an oilfield with large reserves of the highest quality petroleum has improved the outlook of the Republic in this respect. The capital and chief manufacturing centre of the Republic is Minsk (population 950,000). At the 1959 census its population was 509,000 and its extremely rapid growth is accounted for in part by the expansion of its metal-working and machine-building industries.

THE TRANS-CAUCASIAN REPUBLICS

The Republics of Georgia, Azerbaydzhan and Armenia have a total area of 72,000 square miles, somewhat less than that of

the Baltic region. Armenia (11,580 square miles) is the smallest
of all the Union Republics. The conquest of these Caucasus
lands by Russia was completed in 1859. Together they form one
of the economic regions of the USSR with a combined population
of about 13 million. Ethnically the region is extraordinarily
diverse, a fact that is reflected in the administrative structure.
This relatively small area is not only divided into three Republics
for the main nationalities, but there are also five autonomous
republics or *oblasts* for other important ethnic groups. These
diverse peoples inhabit the northern or Great Caucasus mountains, the southern or Little Caucasus range, and the valleys in
between. The Great Caucasus has many awe-inspiring snow-
capped summits, some of them like Mount Elbruz (18,481ft) of
volcanic origin, and the mountains give rise to about 1,400
glaciers, many of them several miles long. Along the Black Sea
coast, where summers are long, hot and humid, there is a
luxuriant sub-tropical vegetation—a mixture of alder, horn-
beam, oak, maple and walnut, with Mediterranean evergreens
like the laurel. But rainfall and snowfall decline rapidly eastwards towards the Caspian Sea, and natural vegetation becomes
scanty and unirrigated agriculture difficult. In the lower valleys,
wherever there is sufficient water, many sub-tropical crops such
as tobacco, citrus fruit, grapes, olives, nuts and even tea are
grown.

The Caucasus region possesses the oldest exploited oilfield in
the world, and industries associated with petroleum have made
the Azerbaydzhan capital, Baku, the largest town in the region
with a 1970 census population of 1,261,000. The region is also
an important producer of copper, manganese, molybdenum,
tungsten and zinc: mining conditions are difficult and the ore
commonly moves from the mountain side by cable car to the
processing plant. After Baku the largest towns are Tbilisi (population 889,000) and Yerevan (767,000), respectively the capitals
of the Georgian and Armenian Republics. The Armenians are
a talented people and this fact has led to an extraordinary expansion of such skill-demanding modern industries as electronics,
machine tools, precision instruments and electrical engineering,

as well as synthetic rubber. Industrialisation is reflected in urbanisation: Yerevan had only 65,000 inhabitants in 1926.

KAZAKHSTAN

The vast Kazakh Republic has an area of over a million square miles, eleven times the size of the whole United Kingdom and four times that of Texas. It corresponds to the extent of grazing land needed by the once nomadic Kazakhs, who migrated to the southern deserts in winter with their flocks, returning northwards in summer. In the late 1950s the steppe lands in the north were ploughed up and sown with wheat, and the immigration of large numbers of Russians and Ukrainians to colonise these newly cultivated lands has meant that now, out of a total population of nearly 13 million, there are more Russians (5½ million) than there are Kazakhs (4 million). There are also almost a million Ukrainians and 200,000 Byelorussians. The Republic is also an economic region.

Almost the whole territory suffers from aridity, and true desert conditions are found in the south around the Caspian and Aral Seas and Lake Balkhash. Here there are extensive irrigation projects, notably along the Syr river, which flows to the Aral Sea, and along the south-eastern borders of the Republic where mountain streams bring fresh water down into the desert. Cotton, wheat, rice, sugar beet, tobacco and fruit are grown on irrigated lands. Some of the Kazakh population are still semi-nomadic, spending long periods away from home with their sheep, and wool is one of the Republic's chief products. Central Kazakhstan has great mineral wealth, including extensive iron ore fields, huge deposits of copper and massive beds of coal. A series of large coal-burning power stations is being constructed on the coalfield and long-distance high-voltage transmission lines will carry the electricity west to Russia. In the remote deserts of Kazakhstan is the Soviet space research station of Baykonyr. The Kazakh capital, Alma Ata (population 750,000), lies in the south-eastern corner of the Republic, close to the frontier with China. Karaganda (530,000), the second largest town, has an important steel works.

Soviet Central Asia consists of four Republics, Uzbekistan, Kirgizstan, Tadzhikstan and Turkmenistan, and forms a single economic region. With a combined area of 476,000 square miles it is over five times the size of Britain or almost ten times as large as New York State. Its population, 20 million at the 1970 census, is the fastest growing in the Soviet Union. This is owing not only to a high rate of natural increase but also to a considerable immigration of people in search of a warm sunny climate. There are 9 million Uzbeks, 3 million Russians, living mostly in the towns, 2 million Tadzhiks, 1½ million Kirgiz, 1½ million Turkmen and a million Tartars. Soviet Central Asia was conquered by the Russians between 1864 and 1884 and the distant province was linked with Russia by railway.

This region has three distinct types of landscape. In the south there are high mountain ranges, most of which are in the Kirgiz and Tadzhik Republics. Hitherto the only economic use of the mountain valleys has been for summer pastures, but now two large hydro-electric stations are being built there, some of the power from which will be used in mineral working.

North of the mountains is a piedmont zone where streams supply irrigation water to fertile loess soils on which most of the Soviet Union's cotton is grown. Some of these lands have been irrigated for a thousand years or more, and ancient ditches are found alongside modern canals and distribution networks; a long extension of productive irrigated land runs north-west from the piedmont along the Amu river to the Aral Sea.

North of the piedmont are the great sand deserts, the Karakum (meaning black sands) and the Kyzylkum (red sands). Through the southern part of the Karakum desert runs the Karakum canal, which takes water from the Amu river to the Turkmenian capital, Ashkhabad (population 260,000), and beyond. It is planned to complete the canal by 1975, when it will have a length of 870 miles and irrigate a million acres of former desert land. Various plants survive the extreme heat, aridity and salinity of the deserts, and in doing so produce certain rare chemical substances which are valuable to man: alkaloids, oils, resins, rubber, tannin, and also drugs such as ephedrine and salzolin, and pesticides such as anabazin.

Besides the produce of their irrigated lands, the Central Asian Republics support large numbers of sheep, some of which yield the highly valued black Karakul fleeces. Mineral wealth is great and varied. There are gasfields, oilfields and coalfields, and two wide-diameter pipelines carry natural gas to central Russia; many metals—gold, iron, copper, manganese, molybdenum and chromite—are also mined. The great city of Tashkent (population 1,400,000), which manufactures agricultural and textile machinery, is the capital of the region and of the Uzbek Republic. A bad earthquake in 1966 destroyed the sprawling mass of adobe huts in which most of the Uzbek population of the city lived, but rebuilding has been rapid and has taken the form of large blocks of flats and new streets of single-family houses, all specially designed to withstand earthquake shocks. Also in Uzbekistan are the cities of Samarkand, Bukhara and Khiva, which retain some of the splendid monuments of their magnificent Moslem past—beautiful mosques, gay minarets, ornate palaces and dignified mausoleums, their walls coated with intricate mosaics of coloured glazed tile. Although they have suffered greatly from past neglect and earthquake damage they have been carefully restored by the Soviet authorities. In the towns of Central Asia, Russians in European dress intermingle with the natives dressed in coloured cottons and silks. The Uzbeks wear distinctive cotton black and white skull caps, a reminder of the fact that their economy is based on cotton, just as the woollen hats of the other Central Asian peoples reflect their dependence on sheep.

E

4

How They Live

LIFE in Russia is very different indeed from that of any advanced Western country. Although statistics are not available, it is clear to any observer that the USSR is relatively free of the violence and crime that threaten the stability of society elsewhere. This is in part attributable to the more authoritarian form of rule, and in part because the population at large do not have access to such aids to crime as cars, drugs and firearms. Furthermore, the educational system, and the powerful propaganda machines of Party and state, continually inculcate the virtues of good citizenship and moral behaviour, and anything that tends to glorify violence is excluded from the television and cinema screens just as guns are banned from the toyshops. When violent crimes do occur drunkenness is the commonest cause. Occasional riots and disturbances also take place for varying reasons in various parts of the far-flung Soviet empire, but the attitude of the majority of people to such demonstrations appears to be passively apathetic if not actively hostile. Soviet society is also free of many of the social pressures to conform, to compete, to make money and to 'succeed' which, spurred on by the seductive advertising of expensive consumer goods, have helped to give some aspects of Western society the name of 'rat race'. While exclusiveness and furnishing of home, style and quality of clothing, and model and date of car have become symbols of status in capitalist countries, such pretensions scarcely exist in Soviet society where all classes share standard apartment houses, wear state-store clothing and ride in public transport.

Soviet life has its disadvantages. The lack of any critical discussion of public affairs and of freedom for political and economic activity, outside the narrow limits prescribed by Party and state, may irk only a few intellectuals or would-be 'business men', but the restrictions on travel abroad, which can usually take place only in supervised groups, must frustrate many more. Those who venture to criticise the basic tenets of the Marxist-Leninist society in which they live, or who question the right of a few men to decide arbitrarily all philosophical, cultural, political and economic issues, may well attract the attention of the secret police. And if they go too far, they may find themselves arraigned for anti-Soviet activities, followed by removal to a mental hospital with release dependent on returning to a 'saner' view.

Life in the USSR also has its darker side in the endless struggle that must be waged against shortage, badly made goods and bureaucratic muddle, the long queues for anything worthwhile, the difficulties of making a simple telephone call or trying to obtain some essential authorisation from some elusive bureaucrat. Such problems have to be seen against the gloomy background of the harsh Russian climate with its long cold dark winter, and the combination of autocratic government, capricious bureaucracy and bitterly cold weather have been fatalistically accepted by ordinary Russians for centuries as their lot in life.

THE FAMILY AND MARRIAGE

Among the 46 per cent of the Soviet population that still inhabits the countryside, what sociologists call the 'extended' family prevails. This consists of not only the marriage pair and their growing children, but also their ageing parents, and possibly their unmarried brothers and sisters, all living in close proximity in one log house or *izba*. Other closely related families live nearby forming a tightly knit village community. In the towns, as in most advanced Western countries, the place of the extended family has been taken by the marriage pair as the basic social unit. This marriage pair tends to live independently of the grandparents and other members of the extended family, who may live hundreds of miles away. Even the children tend to become increasingly independent of their parents. The Party encourages them to join organisations like the Pioneers and the Young Communist League, membership of which necessitates their spending much of their free time away from home; and the state takes them away for compulsory education and military training. The marriage pair often splits through divorce, the rate for which is almost as high in Russia as in America. A notable phenomenon of post-war Russia has been the rise of the boarding school and this has resulted from the high divorce rate and the consequent large numbers of unwanted children. The attitude of the Communist Party towards the family is ambiguous. They support the family because it makes for social stability, yet resent its traditional conservatism. The temptation to reach into the family for the hearts and minds of the children is a very strong one for the more zealous Party members, but in so far as they succeed the family is undermined.

Although most Soviet people accept marriage and register their unions officially at registry offices, little opprobium is attached to those who live together without getting married. To make official marriage more attractive, some ceremonial trappings have been introduced, and to quote the family law for 1971, 'marriage is registered in a ceremonial atmosphere. The registry office ensures a festive atmosphere for the registration of marriages with the consent of the partners to the marriage.'

Divorce is increasing in the USSR with growing urbanisation. In the country as a whole the rate is 2·7 per thousand, but in the towns it is 4·2 per thousand, and in cities with a population over half a million it rises to 4·9 per thousand. Some of the larger urban concentrations have very high rates: 6·0 in Moscow, 5·9 in Leningrad, and 6·3 in Riga and Odessa. A Soviet sociologist, Valentina Perevedentsev, gives as the main causes women's greater economic independence, the fact that in modern urban conditions family life has to compete with interests and friendships connected with one's work and with social activities outside the home, and the growing tolerance shown by society of divorce and sexual relations outside of marriage. The following extracts from Soviet legislation, which came into effect on 1 October 1971, illustrate the present Soviet legal position:

In the lifetime of the two partners a marriage may be dissolved through divorce, by application of either or both partners. A marriage is dissolved by a court. The court takes steps to reconcile the partners to a marriage. A marriage is dissolved if it is established by a court of law that the further joint life of the partners and the preservation of their family have become impossible.

A husband is not entitled, without the consent of his wife, to apply for dissolution of their marriage during the pregnancy of the wife nor in the course of one year after the birth of a child.

When dissolving a marriage, the court, when necessary, takes measures to protect the interests of children under age and of a disabled wife.

A husband and wife who do not have children under age may dissolve a marriage by mutual consent at a registry office.

There is much sexual freedom in the Soviet Union, and sexual relations before and outside of marriage are common. Many young women have had abortions before getting married. Yet there is little discussion of sex, public or private, and nothing of a libidinous or pornographic nature is allowed to be printed, broadcast, filmed or televised for general consumption in the USSR. Sex is not commercially exploited nor is its part in life exaggerated, but it takes its place as a normal and natural function.

Legally women are fully emancipated in Russia: they form over one half of the labour force and have received equal pay since 1917. This is partly a result of Communist ideals, which accept unconditionally the equality of women, but also of the war of 1941–5, which threw a large part of the administrative economic burden upon them. As casualties among the fighting men were so high, women have maintained their dominant position in many branches of the national life since the war.

Thus they make up 85 per cent of those concerned with health and medical care, and most doctors are women. They are also very important in wholesale and retail trade (75 per cent), education and culture (72 per cent), government and administration (58 per cent), manufacturing and mining (47 per cent), scientific activities (46 per cent) and agriculture (43 per cent). Even in the building industry they number over a quarter of the labour force. Nor, as in the West, do they tend to be found mainly in the lower paid or more menial jobs, but occupy many senior positions in the higher administrative, professional and technical labour force. In fact, women account for 60 per cent of all those with higher or specialised education. Of the deputies to the various soviets (elected councils) 43 per cent are female.

Although fully emancipated in society and the national economy Russian women are not so free in the home and family, which are more conservative institutions. In addition to her outside occupation, the Soviet wife is expected to shoulder the household tasks with little help from her husband or from labour-saving devices. Such assistance as she may have is likely to come from her mother or her husband's mother—a *babushka* or grandmother. Because of heavy wartime losses, a very large proportion of the elderly women of Russia are widows. With a stubborn patience born of the harsh experiences of a lifetime afflicted by revolution and war, terror and famine, these women will stand for hours in queues, making it possible for the family to obtain little luxuries that would otherwise escape them.

Russian communists boast that children are the privileged class in the Soviet Union, and Lenin's remark that 'everything we have done . . . in the final analysis is for them, for the children' is often quoted. There is some truth in the claim, as evidenced by the priority given to the young in many goods and services in short supply. Some of the first acts of the new Bolshevik government were to protect children—none were to be employed under the age of 14, those aged 14 were limited to four hours' work a day, and those under 15 who were needy could claim free meals. Most newborn babies are breast-fed and much care and affection is lavished upon them.

STANDARD OF LIVING

The material level of living in a country depends upon the size of personal incomes and the availability of goods and services. Personal incomes in the USSR amount to some 40 per cent of the total national income, and the average wage in industry in 1970 was about 1,500 roubles a year. This is a great deal less than that received by the American worker (about 5,800 roubles) and considerably less than the British worker—about 3,255 roubles. But in the Western countries much more of the wage-earner's income goes to direct taxation, housing and transport and, in the United States, to medical care. Fifty-four per cent of the American employee's pay goes on such outlays compared with only 10 per cent of the Russian's.

Average incomes mean little unless the actual distribution is taken into account. This is much more uneven in most capitalist countries. Thus whereas in the USA the most highly paid 10 per cent of the population receives some 30 times as much as the lowest paid 10 per cent, in the USSR the top 10 per cent receives only between 3 or 4 times as much. The most highly remunerated are the top Party leaders and administrators, after whom come those who have made successful careers in the professions and the arts. These may earn as much as 12,000 roubles a year. Below these come leading engineers and technicians, and the managers of factories, who get between 4,000 and 2,500 roubles. Then come the various grades of skilled workers, with between 2,000 and 1,200 roubles, and then the unskilled workers, with between 1,200 and 900 roubles. Most ordinary collective farmers get even less—about 500 roubles, although skilled and specialist grades in farming earn considerably more. Real wages are constantly rising, however, and doubled between 1950 and 1970.

It is not so much low incomes that restrict the standard of living of the average Russian worker as the non-availability or short supply of wanted goods in the shops. Because of the priority long given to heavy industry, consumers' goods are deficient in quality, quantity and range. There are large stocks of unsold or unsaleable articles in Russian shops alongside queues for scarce items in great demand. The difficulty in obtaining many goods is more a matter of bad distribution than of actual deficiency in supply. Thus most articles are more plentiful in Moscow than elsewhere, and the capital gives a more favourable idea of the goods available to the public than would be true of the country as a whole. As a result Moscow is invaded by a large number of provincials seeking goods unavailable at home. However, the narrower range of available goods is not felt so keenly by the Russian as it would be by the Western shopper, because the psychological pressures of powerful advertising are not there to create new and to stimulate existing wants.

HOUSING

Before the Revolution most Russians, both in town and country, lived in primitive wooden houses which, although often attractive from the outside because of their lovingly carved and ornate window frames, were provided inside with no plumbing and only the crudest furnishings. In the towns these wooden houses were arranged along unpaved streets which consisted of churned-up mud in spring and autumn, before and after the winter freezing. In the central parts of the larger towns there were some brick buildings of two or three storeys which were divided up into flats. The Soviet period has seen a severe housing shortage because it has coincided with a massive shift of the population from the countryside to the towns, but the problem was exacerbated by the devastation wrought by the 1941–5 war The authorities have gone some way to meet the problem by adopting modern techniques in the rapid assembly of large apartment houses from prefabricated panels, and by keeping the size of apartment allocated to the average family very small. The result is that, whereas in most advanced Western countries there is, on an average, one person or less to a room, in the

USSR there are two people to a room. Nevertheless, the present situation is a great improvement on the recent past when most urban families had to live in a single room and use a communal kitchen and bathroom. At present everyone is entitled to 12 square metres (just over 14 square yards) of living space, which would amount to two rooms, each 11ft square, for a childless couple, plus kitchen and bathroom. The target of a minimum of one room, a bed-sitter, together with private kitchen and bathroom, for every family is being achieved by a building programme of enormous proportions. But two-room flats (living room and bedroom) now form a large proportion of Soviet housing, and there is a relatively small percentage of three-roomed apartments. This improvement has been effected to a large extent by building taller blocks. During the 1950s, when the need was most desperate because of wartime destruction and rapid urbanisation, standard five-storey blocks without lifts were erected with little regard for quality or design. Now buildings of up to twenty-five storeys are being built and some attention to style and diversification is attempted. In Moscow the ground-floor of such high-rise buildings provides services for the tenants—shops, cafés and restaurants, hairdressers and a cinema.

Most town-dwellers seem content with their new self-contained flats despite their small size and often poor workmanship. This is because they are such an improvement upon the wooden *izba* or the communal apartment house from which they have moved, and because the rents are so low, amounting to only about 5 per cent of the household's income, and inclusive of hot water, electricity and gas. To give an actual instance from Moscow, four people, inhabiting a two-room furnished flat (with kitchen and bathroom) equipped with hot and cold water, electricity, refrigerator, television and telephone, pay a monthly rent of 11 roubles inclusive of everything but the telephone bill. The standard apartment houses are built by the local authorities, but they do not provide all housing. Factory managements also build blocks of flats to attract skilled workers, and the terms are then even more favourable. Those who wish and can afford it may build their own houses, and the wealthier people take advantage of this by building summer houses—*dachas*—in the country. There are also co-operative housing associations which build flats for private sale—usually with payment spread over a period of years. The authorities, far from disapproving of this practice, encourage it by lending these associations the necessary funds. Such apartments are expensive, however—from about 2,000 roubles for a single room to 7,000 for three rooms—and only within reach of the higher paid.

Furniture in the average apartment is plain and confined to essentials, there seldom being room for much besides table, chairs, bookshelf and sideboard. Radios and televisions are universal, and in the towns the number of refrigerators, vacuum cleaners and telephones is rising rapidly.

FOOD AND DRINK

In some respects the Russian diet is similar to that of western Europe fifty years ago, before the food-processing and packaging revolution. Bread, cabbage, potatoes and fish are regular ingredients, meat is expensive and often scarce and many vegetables and fruits are only available seasonally. The range of foodstuffs on sale is much narrower than in Britain or America, as food imports from other parts of the world are on a much smaller scale. Foods are normally purchased in their natural or raw state, and all the preparation and cooking is done at home. This places a considerable burden on the women, who are expected to produce the meals even though they usually have jobs outside. In addition they have the problem of shopping for food which, in the state stores, often involves selecting the item after waiting one's turn, paying for it at the cash desk after waiting in another queue, and then joining a third queue with one's receipt in order to claim the goods. Shopping is simpler for women who have access to a collective farmers' market. Collective farmers who live within reach of towns are free to sell their surplus produce in urban markets, but such supplies are seasonal—plentiful and varied in summer, but almost non-existent in winter.

Many Russians have their main meal in works canteens where the food is cheap and adequate; and, as wages have risen faster than consumer goods have become available in the shops, more and more people feel they can afford to dine out, with the result that long queues develop outside the overcrowded restaurants in the evenings. The CPSU recognises the need to improve the methods of retailing food, and the service in restaurants and canteens. In February 1972 it was announced that the Central Committee of the Communist Party and the Soviet government had agreed on 'far-reaching measures to improve shops, catering establishments, factory canteens, collective farm markets and the entire system of retail trade in the USSR'. It was stated that an improvement in retail trade was 'an important precondition for raising the living and cultural standards of the Soviet people', and also that it was intended to introduce self-service methods on a wide scale.

Russians tend to need and eat more substantial meals, rich in carbohydrates, than Westerners: heavy manual labour still plays a large part in their economy; few have cars and they therefore walk more; and they often live and work in relatively cold conditions. The USSR has a great variety of regional culinary specialities. This is because it has such a variety of climates and soils, causing the produce available to the cook to differ from place to place; because there are so many different races and nationalities, each with its own food customs; and because Russia has had long periods of contact with so many different countries of Asia and Europe—India, China, Persia, France, Germany, Italy and Britain, to mention but a few.

In Russia proper many distinctive tasty and nourishing soups are made. They are usually vegetable soups with whatever meat or fish is available added. *Shchy* is a cabbage or sauerkraut soup with some turnip, carrot, onion or leek and perhaps beef. *Borshch* is a beetroot soup, again with vegetables and meat, and which, like so many Russian dishes, contains sour cream or *smetana*; in summer it is served cold instead of hot and has egg instead of meat. *Smetana* is one of the commonest ingredients in Russian cooking; it is the basis of many sauces and it is often used in making cakes or puddings. *Solyanka* is another favourite soup. The main ingredient is meat or fish, but it may also have cucumbers, tomatoes, onions, olives, capers, lemon, butter and, of course, *smetana*.

Mushrooms, potatoes and cabbage, all plentiful in Russia, are eaten in a variety of dishes. Beef Stroganov is the most famous of Russian ways of preparing meat. The beef, cut into small slices, is first fried and then simmered with mushrooms and onion, and the inevitable *smetana* added. In Soviet Central Asia and the Caucasus, where the sheep is the traditional animal, mutton *shashliks* can still be seen being cooked on wooden skewers over open fires; they are eaten with boiled rice. Caviar is a delicacy which belongs to Russia, but the less expensive red caviar or salmon roe is more common than the black variety, the true caviar or roe of the sturgeon.

Many Russian foods are based on cereals. Bread, especially rye bread, is a staple article of the national diet. Often all that peasants had to eat in hungry days was *kasha*, a boiled buckwheat porridge, sometimes eaten with *smetana* and cream cheese or butter. Then there are Russian pancakes or *bliny*, made with flour, milk, eggs, butter and yeast, and often eaten with caviar, smoked salmon or *smetana*. Dumplings are found in many soups. Pies or *pirogi*, the pastry made with yeast dough, have many tasty fillings, which may be vegetable such as cabbage, rice, mushrooms, etc, or meat, poultry or fish.

Russian soups and salads are not just introductory courses but big meals in themselves, such is the profusion and volume of the ingredients. As Musia Soper writes in her little book, *Cooking the Russian Way*:

Perhaps Russian meals may be considered to be too substantial and to take more time to prepare than the modern housewife is willing to give, but the cooking on the whole is suitable for their climate which, over a large area, has long cold winters calling for substantial dishes: filling soups, rich fish and meat dishes, and as a prelude to these, their

famous zakusky (hors d'oeuvre) accompanied, perhaps, by a glass of
vodka to warm a guest before the start of the main meal.

Tea and mineral water are the commonest drinks, and
although coffee, cocoa and chocolate are available, less of these
is drunk than in Britain or America. Tea is always served with
sugar, which is sometimes placed in the mouth to sweeten the
liquid as it is drunk, is commonly taken with lemon, and only
occasionally with milk. In hot weather the refreshing *kvas*, a
non-alcoholic drink made from grain or surplus bread, is sold
from roadside tanks. Beer, wine and spirits—both vodka and
brandy—are also widely drunk and, despite state propaganda
against drunkenness, its extent gives cause for concern. Many
good wines are produced, notably 'Soviet champagne', which
comes from Georgia and is regularly drunk on festive occasions
and often by ladies when the men are drinking vodka.

Food prices are high, so that Russians may spend up to half
their income on food, compared with an average of less than a
quarter in Britain or America.

CLOTHING

Clothing in the USSR still tends to be unexciting in style and
poor in quality, and foreign tourists are often approached with
offers to buy clothes. Russian visitors to Britain are keen to take
back high-quality woollens. The emphasis on industrialising the
country as rapidly as possible meant that, for much of the Soviet
period, little attention was paid to the textile and clothing industries, which, starved of capital investment and talent, produced only the bare necessities, and these were often drab and
shoddy. The past few years have seen a considerable improvement in the range, style and quality of clothing. But there is still
little variety, styles tend to be old-fashioned, and high-quality
goods are rare.

As in the West, those occupying administrative, professional
and managerial posts dress in lounge suits, both men and women,

while men of the working class wear open-necked cotton shirts indoors, with perhaps a jacket; their women wear cotton prints with jumpers or cardigans. Man-made fibres are not yet much in evidence. In the larger cities, however, young women wearing well-made fashionable clothes are becoming increasingly apparent, and the contrast between them and the older women, attired in headscarves and cheap, shapeless, drab old clothes, is a striking one. In winter fur-collared overcoats, fur hats and fur-lined boots are standard wear in the towns. Young people are neatly and tidily dressed without the extravagant styles or careless abandon often seen in the West. School children wear neat uniforms and carry the standard briefcase as do older students and officials. In the summer the boy scout/girl guide uniform of the Young Pioneers, worn with two-cornered red hats, is commonly seen; and the national costumes of the very many nationalities of the USSR give to holidays and parades a colourful variety absent from the everyday scene.

Prices of Russian clothing are very high, especially in view of the quality. A suit of clothes may cost a hundred roubles or a month's wages for many industrial workers, and some estimates attribute 40 per cent of personal expenditure to clothing. The harsh climatic conditions are partly responsible, making abundant warm clothing a necessity. Children's clothing, on the other hand, is cheap, being heavily subsidised.

SOCIAL SERVICES

Medical and dental care are free of charge in the USSR although sometimes the patient may have to buy his own drugs. There are no contributions deducted from salaries or wages. Medical staff are attached to all large enterprises and it is normal for a worker to consult his factory doctor if there is anything wrong with him. The free medical service includes hospital treatment and recuperation in sanatoria. These, usually located near pleasure resorts such as those on the Black Sea Coast, are often the converted mansions of former wealthy aristocrats, and many of them are run by various industrial undertakings and trade unions. If the factory doctor advises it, the worker's trade union will arrange for his or her visit. Workers away ill get their full wages if they have been in employment continuously for eight years, and 80 per cent of their pay if they have between five and eight years' service. Thus, but the time they are in their late twenties almost all Soviet workers qualify for the full benefit. In 1970 the state spent 9 billion roubles on the health service.

The Soviet Union has a generous system of maternity benefits and family allowances. Women receive maternity leave before and after childbirth on full pay, irrespective of the length of time they have been working. Women who are on their own— unmarried, widowed, divorced or deserted—receive extra allowances. Non-contributory old-age pensions are paid to all at the age of 60 for men and 55 for women. The rate varies, according to length and type of service, from a minimum of 30 roubles a month to a maximum of 120 roubles, while for collective farmers there are lower rates: a minimum of 12 roubles a month to a maximum of 102 roubles. Handicapped persons and fatherless families also receive welfare payments. There is no unemployment pay because there is a continuing labour shortage in the USSR and it is assumed that everyone who wants a job can get it, although it may not be the kind of work he would prefer or be best qualified to do. There were no labour exchanges until 1969, when they were set up to help people find the kind of employment they were looking for.

COUNTRY LIFE

The Revolution of 1917 was made in the cities of Russia by urban factory workers and their leaders. Although the peasantry welcomed the opportunity it gave them to seize the estates of the gentry, they subsequently showed little enthusiasm for communist ideology and were reluctant to supply free food to the towns, for in the chaotic economic conditions of the early Soviet period, the townsmen had little to offer by way of payment. In the late 1920s and early 1930s Stalin effected a massive re-organisation of Russian agriculture, replacing the peasant holdings with mechanised collective farms. These farms had to deliver fixed quotas of produce to the state in order to feed the towns, and payment for these deliveries was very low. The farms did not have control over the necessary machinery but were dependent on state-controlled machine-tractor stations. As a result, while the urban standard of living steadily improved, the peasantry were kept in a state of deprivation and poverty. They continued to live in primitive log huts without piped water, plumbing or electricity and they remained without the various amenities which became increasingly the prerogative of the city dweller: shops, restaurants, nurseries, kindergartens, laundries, hospitals, and higher educational and cultural opportunities. A great gulf developed between life in the town and life in the country.

From 1960 on, the CPSU has made the abolition of this gulf one of its main aims, but although narrower than it was, and lessening with each year that passes, the difference remains, and as almost half the population of the Soviet Union is rural, it affects 100 million people. Incomes on the farms have risen dramatically during the past decade, but they remain well below

---

The first day of September begins a new school year and these children have just started primary school. Young school-children wear a standard black and white uniform. Girls' hair is often plaited, but boys have it shorn close to the head.

Students at a lecture in the great auditorium of Moscow University. Degrees are the key to a better-paid and more comfortable life, but the competition is keen and the strain great.

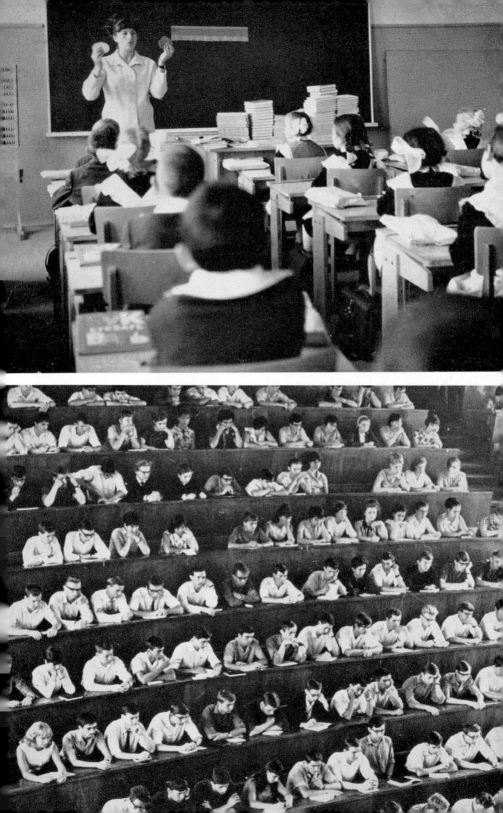

those of the towns. A guaranteed minimum wage for agricultural workers was introduced in 1965, but it is lower than the industrial minimum. Nevertheless, this was a great step forward, as some badly located or poorly run farms were scarcely able to pay their workers enough to keep them from starving. Now the state lends such farms enough money to pay the minimum wage. Pensions and other social security payments were extended to the farms in 1964, but at lower rates than in the towns. Most collective farms have built clubs, nurseries and kindergartens, and many are building bakeries, laundries and canteens, and are striving to provide other amenities, but the countryman is still far worse off in this respect than the townsman. Most farms generate their own electricity, but many houses are not connected to the farm supply and few have piped water. The village well remains their main source of supply. Collective farmers, unlike workers in industry, have to have passports and cannot leave the farm's employ without permission. This is to keep the movement into the towns within manageable levels. Its effect is weakened by the exemption given to young men after they have done their military service. As a result they often do not return to the farm.

The agricultural worker is not so badly off as mere statistics of income, pensions, etc would imply. Life in the village is more

---

The railway is the main mode of conveyance for both passengers and goods. This train has just set down hundreds of Muscovites at a summer-cottage resort station. In the absence of large numbers of private cars, the passengers are representative of all ranks of society.

A large proportion of the Soviet Union's private cars are concentrated in Moscow, where they compete more and more with lorries and public transport for road space. Although the streets of the capital are wide, congestion is increasing.

F

cohesive. There is mutual help to a degree unknown in the towns. Large families work together as well as live together, and although individual incomes may be lower than in the towns, the collective household income may be larger. Social security benefits need not be so high for those living with and supported by their families in the traditional rural manner as for those compelled to live on their own in urban conditions. Furthermore, the collective farmer has his private plot, a smallholding on which he and his family grow their own food, and keep chickens, a couple of pigs perhaps, and a cow. Life in the country has other compensations. It preserves much of the fun and gaiety of traditional customs, such as the festivities which celebrate the arrival of spring.

The Party's favourite plan for reducing the gulf between town and country has been to replace the old scattered and isolated villages of log houses by small central towns, in which urban amenities could be the more readily provided. For this reason collective farms were amalgamated until their populations were large enough to support small towns of a few thousand inhabitants, and as a result, they are extremely large, averaging 15,000 acres. But until recently there was such opposition amongst the peasantry to the idea of the 'agrotown' that little progress was made. The old generation of peasants clung obstinately to their old *izbas*: but today attitudes are changing, and although there is still a widespread preference for single dwelling houses, many young collective farmers, and particularly their wives, welcome the idea of a well-appointed flat in a new block. Now collective farms are developing central townships, using both blocks of flats and single houses, and allowing some of the old villages to decay.

The introduction of the agrotown has two further advantages. The vast Russian territory is poorly supplied with surfaced roads, and many villages are inaccessible to motor traffic, especially in the muddy seasons of spring and autumn. Whereas it would be out of the question to build a road system to serve every village, it is a more practicable proposition to build one to the central township. The second advantage of the agrotown is that it helps solve the problem of the enforced idleness which the Russian climate imposes upon much of the rural population in winter. The new rural township will have a labour force large enough to support a factory, and many collectives are now building their own industrial establishments, usually to process their own produce. These enable the inhabitants to work part of the year in the factory and part in the field, thus not only raising their own incomes, but increasing the profitability of the farm.

LIFE IN THE NORTH

Life is particularly harsh in the northernmost parts of the USSR where winter may last for nine months and there is no real summer. For several weeks there is scarcely any daylight and the subsoil is permanently frozen. Wages double those paid in central Russia have not sufficed to attract enough labour to these regions and the Soviet government has had to go to great lengths in improving living conditions in the tundra zone. Near the Arctic city of Norilsk an immense building is being erected to house 1,000 people in 220 capacious flats. Their windows and balconies look inwards to a central courtyard which is roofed in with transparent plastic and which is maintained at a temperature of 60°F. The 500ft long block includes a club, cinema, library, clinic, school, kindergarten, and many other facilities, so that the inhabitants will seldom have to leave their artificial environment. Such enclosed villages are planned for other sites and offer a much more comfortable life for those who have to live within the Arctic Circle.

5

How They Work

BECAUSE of the contrasting structure of their economies and different methods of accounting it is impossible to make a reliable comparison between the 'gross national product' or total productivity of the USSR and of the leading capitalist countries. Most authorities estimate the Soviet figure to be about half that of the United States or four times that of the United Kingdom. Such estimates are unrealistic because the national product of non-communist countries is swollen by many items which have no place in the Soviet economy. Thus the Soviet system attaches much less importance to finance, banking and insurance, while such activities as advertising and commercial litigation, which loom large in the American or British gross national product, are irrelevant to the Soviet economy. The Soviets claim that their industrial production, including both mining and manufacturing, amounts by value to 70 per cent of that of the United States, their agricultural production to 85 per cent, and the freight carried by their transport system to 96 per cent of the American total. What is beyond doubt is that industrial production in the USSR has expanded very rapidly during the Soviet period: it more than doubled during the 1960s and has multiplied over ten times since the end of the war in 1945. The most remarkable feature of Soviet industrial output is the large proportion which comes from heavy industry. Much more so than in all Western countries, Russian industry works to increase the stock of capital goods—mines, power stations, factories, machinery, etc, and places less emphasis on the production of finished goods for the consumer.

THE LABOUR FORCE

The Soviet labour force totals about 110 million as against 78 million in the USA. As total production is considerably greater in America, this means that productivity per worker is much lower in the USSR. There are several reasons for this: Soviet industry is less highly mechanised and automated; the average working week is the shortest amongst advanced countries; because everyone must be given a job many workers are found employment for whom there is not really much to do, or who are not really suitable and who would fail to get work in countries where employers have greater freedom to dismiss workers than do enterprises in the USSR; finally, the hard Russian winter interrupts outdoor work to a great extent and thus lessens productivity.

The Russian labour force is distinguished by the large proportion engaged in agriculture—about 25 per cent compared with under 5 per cent in America and even less in Britain. Among individual industries the leading employer, after agriculture, is the machine-building and metal-working industry, employing over 9 million workers, followed by the textile industry (4·2 million), the food-processing industry (2·4 million), the building materials industry (1·7 million), chemicals (1·2 million), iron and steel (1·1 million) and coal mining (1 million). The importance of women in the labour force at all levels has already been noted: one half of all workers are women.

Wage rates are differently based from those in the West, where they depend upon a combination of social tradition, the profitability of the industry, supply related to demand, qualifications or skills required and the ability of the trade union to apply pressure. In Russia wages are determined by what is called the 'socialist value of labour'. This is calculated by taking into account the value of the industry to the economy, the geographical location (with higher rates in the remoter, harsher parts of the country), the working conditions (with higher rates where these are difficult or unpleasant) and the degree of skill or qualification required. Such considerations establish a 'norm' above which large bonuses can be earned by above-average productivity.

The average length of the working week is about forty hours, but some industries work shorter hours because of difficult, dangerous or unhealthy conditions. Thus, in coal mining the average is thirty-eight hours: overtime is forbidden except in emergencies and then only with the consent of the trade union. Coal miners, in fact, receive many compensations for the unpleasant nature of their task. Where technical conditions permit, a hot mid-day meal of soup, steak and fried egg, with coffee, is brought to the face: workers who have spent twenty years or more underground can retire on pension at fifty, but they may go on working if they choose and draw their pension as well as their pay. The pension is 60 per cent of their wages, subject to a maximum of 120 roubles a month.

Absenteeism is dealt with by putting the culprit's name in the wall newspaper or publicly criticising him at the union meeting: he will draw no pay for the time he does not work, and he will lose his chance of a bonus and other benefits.

CAPITAL EQUIPMENT

The labour force uses capital equipment, mainly in the form of industrial buildings and machinery, to transform materials into desired goods. All capital equipment in the USSR is publicly owned, and unlike that of most Western countries, it is constantly being worked to full capacity. For whereas the chief problem for most industrialised countries is to find full employment for their plant and workers, the overriding task in the USSR is to meet the demands of an expanding economy from inadequate facilities. Generally speaking plant in Russia takes longer to erect and works less efficiently than in Western countries, and Brezhnev complained to the 1971 meeting of the Communist

Party Congress that 'the number of unfinished projects grows' and that 'the quality of construction remains poor'.

A country's position in the industrial world depends on its ability to advance technologically. Whereas most industrial research abroad is carried out by private companies, in Russia it is mainly the function of the Academy of Sciences, and the application of the resulting technology is a matter for the government departments which administer the various industries. Generally these departments and the enterprises working under them do not welcome innovations. They are eager to fulfil or exceed the planned output target, and the introduction of new technology, however beneficial in the long run, is likely to disrupt production in the short term. Although in some sectors— eg space research, military equipment, aircraft—Soviet technology is ahead of American, in others it lags some ten to twenty years behind. Unlike West Germany and Japan, Russia did not use the opportunity of wartime devastation to modernise her industrial equipment. Instead Stalin insisted on reconstructing industry much as it had been before the war.

ENERGY

Since the industrial revolution, man has relied upon increasing amounts of energy derived from fossil fuels to drive his machinery and transport his goods. Oil (40 per cent) and gas (20 per cent) now provide most energy in the USSR, but coal (31 per cent) remains important and hydro-electricity supplies an additional 6 per cent. The remaining 3 per cent comes from the burning of wood and peat.

OIL AND GAS

The oilfields around Baku were the most productive in the world in the early days of petroleum production, but as no further significant discoveries were made, Russia fell back from first place in 1900 to third in 1950. Since then three great new oilfields have been brought into large-scale production—the Volga-Urals, the Kazakh and the West Siberian. As a result the Soviet Union, with a production of 372 million metric tons in 1971, occupies a position close behind the United States and far ahead of any other country.

In natural gas also the discovery and development of vast new fields in the 1960s have transformed Russia from a relatively unimportant producer of gas in 1950 to second place only to the United States in 1970. Her reserves are now thought to be unmatched by those of any other country. The chief gasfields are in the Arctic tundra, Soviet Central Asia, the North Caucasus and the Ukraine. A network of wide-diameter pipelines is being built to bring the gas to central Russia and also to export it to Europe. Not only do the communist countries of eastern Europe depend on the Soviet Union for gas, but agreements have also been made recently to supply West Germany, Austria, France and Italy.

COAL

The USSR is estimated to hold two-thirds of the world's coal reserves, but the bulk of these lie in eastern Siberia and are too inaccessible to compete with other sources at present. The 1971 production of 641 million metric tons was greater than that of any other country, although much of the production is low grade and lignite. The leading coalfield remains that of the Donets basin (Donbass) in the Ukraine. This is one of the great coalfields of the world and ranks with the Northern Appalachian coalfield in the USA and the Ruhr coalfield in West Germany. Its annual production of over 200 million metric tons exceeds the combined production of all the British coalfields. Much of the coal won is good coking coal, but the seams are difficult and costly to work. By contrast, in the second most productive coalfield, that of northern Kazakhstan, the coal lies in great masses, easy and cheap to exploit mechanically. Here the annual production of over 100 million tons a year will rise rapidly as the large coal-burning electric power stations being built on the field come into production.

In electrical generating capacity and production, the USSR comes second to the USA. Output in 1971 was 800 billion kWh. Most power stations are thermal and burn coal, lignite, gas, oil and even peat. In addition to generating electricity they supply the towns with hot water, which is piped into the apartment houses. About 20 per cent of production comes from hydro-electric stations. These are found on many of the country's rivers, notably on the Volga, Dnieper, Yenisey and its tributary the Angara. Some of the Siberian stations are extremely powerful and that at Krasnoyarsk is the largest in the world (capacity 6 million kW). That being built at Shushensk on the Yenisey will be even larger than Krasnoyarsk (6·4 million kW). The largest hydro-electric station in the United States is at present the Moses Niagara on the Niagara river (capacity 2 million kW).

There is also a large nuclear energy programme. Medium-sized nuclear power stations already operate at Voronezh in southern Russia (present capacity 0·6 million kW) and in the Urals at Beloyarsk (0·3 million kW). In 1971 Kosygin told the Party Congress: 'During the coming five years we shall launch a broad programme for the building of atomic power stations, chiefly in the European part of the country, where fuel resources are limited. This programme envisages the commissioning, over the next ten to twelve years, of atomic power stations with a total capacity of 30 million kW.' The American programme is similar and should have a capacity of 32 million kW by the end of the 1970s.

METALS

The Soviet Union has vast resources of almost every industrial metal. She produces over twice as much iron ore (203 million metric tons) as any other country. In an average year she also holds first place in the production of chromium, lead, magnesite, manganese and platinum; second place in beryllium, cadmium, copper, gold, magnesium, nickel, titanium, tungsten, vanadium and zinc; and comes third in output of bauxite, mercury, molybdenum and silver. The great iron-ore mining districts are in the Ukraine at Krivoy Rog, in the Urals and in northern Kazakhstan. Immense deposits of copper have also been found in Kazakhstan. International mining companies are becoming increasingly interested in the great and often hitherto untouched reserves of metals in Siberia and Kazakhstan, and negotiations are proceeding between some of them and the Soviet government for their joint exploitation.

OTHER MINERALS

Among the many other minerals in the production of which the Soviet Union occupies a prominent position are asbestos (2nd in world rank), china clay (3rd), diamonds (2nd), diatomite (2nd), feldspar (2nd), fluorspar (2nd), graphite (3rd), mica (1st), potash (1st), salt (3rd) and sulphur (2nd) .

STEEL

The iron and steel industry is the basis of a country's industrial strength. Output of steel has risen steadily by a planned amount of 4 to 5 million metric tons a year for the past twenty years and in 1971 the Soviet Union, with a production of 121 million metric

tons, surpassed the United States for the first time. In 1950
Russian production was less than a third of the American.
But the capacity of the United States industry is far greater: it
could probably produce 175 million tons of steel a year if required, whereas the Soviet production is the maximum that
can be obtained from existing capacity. Soviet steel output is
made up of much heavier and thicker articles than is that of
Western countries. In America, Japan, Germany and Britain
the motor industry is the steel industry's chief customer; hence
most steel in those countries is made into flat-rolled products as
opposed to the heavy castings which constitute the bulk of
Russian output. Furthermore, because planned targets in the
USSR are by weight there is a temptation to go for bulk in the
Soviet industry. But in Western countries the steel industry, to
remain competitive, cannot afford to waste material and has to
make its steels as light as possible, consistent with strength, in
order to compete with aluminium and plastics. Size is a feature
of the Soviet industry. Being but a single organisation with a vast
market at its command it can make full use of economies of scale,
and the largest capacity blast furnaces in the world are to be
found at its steelworks in the Ukraine and the Urals.

MACHINE BUILDING AND METAL WORKING

Most of the steel produced is consumed by the metal-working
and machine-building industries. Volume of production in these
industries is comparable to that of the United States, and takes
place in very many centres across the country, but more
especially in and around Moscow, and at Leningrad, Kiev,
Kharkov, Gorkiy, Sverdlovsk, Minsk and Tashkent. Quality and
technology vary remarkably. In some aspects, eg in the use of
metal-forming machinery, the Russians are well behind the
Americans, while in others, notably electrical and electro-
chemical methods of machining, they are ahead.

The biggest contrast between Russia and the West is to be
found in the position of the motor industry. Whereas in America,

West Germany, Britain, France, Italy and Japan it is the leading engineering industry, in the USSR it is relatively unimportant. In 1971 production of all motor vehicles was just over a million, with private cars accounting for only 529,000. This nevertheless, was a big increase on 1970 when only 344,000 cars were made. Production of cars in America is about 8 million a year, in West Germany 3½ million, in France 2 million, in Britain 1¾ million, in Italy 1½ million and in Canada 1 million. On the other hand, the Soviet Union produces more railway locomotives and rolling stock than any other country, a result of the fact that rail transport is far more important than motor transport in Russia.

The Soviet automotive industry is not concentrated in one centre as at Detroit. Motor vehicles are made at several places, but the largest car plant is the new one built by Fiat for the Soviet government at Tolyatti on the Volga near Kuybyshev. The largest lorry/truck plant in the world is under construction, again with foreign assistance, at Chelniy on the Kama river— an indication of increased Russian interest in motor transport.

If the Soviet motor industry is relatively unimportant the same cannot be said of the aircraft industry. Production data are not available, but it supplies the Soviet airline Aeroflot, the largest in the world, with all its aeroplanes, as well as producing for the air force and industry. It also has a growing export market. Its technology is advanced and Russia was the first country to fly a supersonic passenger air liner.

Shipbuilding has a somewhat similar history to motor production. It was relatively neglected until the late 1960s, but then began to expand rapidly to supply ships to a growing merchant marine and navy. The Russians had previously relied upon foreign vessels to carry much of their trade.

ALUMINIUM

The Soviet Union, with an annual output of well over 1 million tons of aluminium, comes second only to the USA,, and possesses the largest single smelter. This is located at Krasnoyarsk in East

Siberia and uses electricity from the giant hydro-electric power station there. The USSR uses domestic supplies of bauxite, nepheline and alunite as ore, but also imports some bauxite and alumina (aluminium oxide extracted from bauxite) for its smelters. Aluminium is not so widely used in Russia as in the West. Some of its main uses—for car engines, lorry/truck bodies and wrapping materials—are not important in Russia, where the aircraft industry is the chief consumer. Consequently over a third of Soviet aluminium is exported.

CHEMICALS

Until the 1960s this was a backward industry in the Soviet Union, but during that decade it received heavy investment in a long overdue attempt to catch up in the production of synthetic fibres, plastics and agricultural chemicals. The petrochemical industry in particular has undergone rapid expansion as new and productive oilfields have been opened up, and complete factories have been purchased abroad. Nevertheless, Soviet production of synthetic resins and plastics is still well below that of the leading Western nations.

BUILDING MATERIALS

Because of the rapid industrial development of the country and the housing drive, the Soviet Union produces more cement bricks, glass, etc than any other country, including America.

TEXTILES

In tsarist times the textile industry was Russia's leading manufacture and it still provides almost all the textile materials and clothing required for a population of nearly 250 million, imports being small. Its products are chiefly of cotton, linen, wool and natural silk, and it differs from Western industries in the comparatively small role played by man-made fibres. The industry developed in the nineteenth century in and around Moscow where most of the mills are still located, but new ones have been established on the Volga and in Soviet Central Asia.

AGRICULTURE

For several reasons agriculture has proved a constant thorn in the flesh of the Soviet leaders. The production of crops and livestock cannot be planned, controlled and increased in the same way as can industrial goods, being largely at the mercy of the weather and subject to local variation of soils and other natural conditions. In an industry in which local knowledge is all important centralised planning by distant bureaucrats can be disastrous. Also, because of the policy of enforced collectivisation put into effect by Stalin before the war, much ill-feeling was caused in the countryside, and the older generation of farmers, nostalgic for the independence of private ownership and control of their land, failed to co-operate fully.

The Soviet leaders may be expecting the impossible in asking that Soviet farmers produce enough food for a population of nearly 250 million, a population that is growing in number and demanding a better diet. For the USSR is, on the whole, a cool northerly land: most of it lies to the north of the fiftieth parallel whereas the United States lies wholly south of that latitude. Those parts of the Soviet Union that do extend farther south, mainly in Soviet Central Asia, are either too dry or too mountainous for farming. It is generally true that those areas of the country that are warm enough for agriculture are too dry and those that are wet enough are too cold. Despite the great size of the country, so much of it is barren tundra, dense forest, undrained swamp, arid desert or steeply mountainous that cultivable land is not so extensive as one might expect. Although comparisons are commonly made with agriculture in America, such comparisons are bound to be unfavourable.

In 1950 the area of cropland in the United States was considerably greater than in the Soviet Union, but since then the American total has declined to about 300 million acres and the Russian has increased to over 500 million acres. This is because, while in America overproduction has led to much land going out of cultivation, in the USSR more and more marginal land has been brought under the plough in order to meet the elusive planned production targets. In the late 1950s Khrushchev organised the ploughing up of a vast extent of virgin steppe land in northern Kazakhstan which had hitherto been considered too dry for agriculture. Irrigation is being continually expanded in the arid lands of Soviet Central Asia, thus adding further to the total of cultivable land. Far-reaching plans to reverse some of the water which the Siberian river Ob carries northwards to the Arctic Ocean, and bring it southwards to the deserts around the Caspian Sea, will make possible a further large extension of the irrigated land.

From her 500 million acres the USSR in 1971 produced 181 million metric tons of grain (USA 230 million tons), 72 million tons of sugar beet (USA 23 million tons), 92 million tons of potatoes (USA 14 million tons), 20 million tons of other vegetables, 7 million tons of raw cotton and 6 million tons of sunflower seeds. In addition Soviet livestock yielded 83 million metric tons of milk (USA 55 million), 13 million tons of meat (USA 16 million), 424,000 tons of wool (little wool is produced in America) and 45 billion eggs (USA 71 billion). Sheep and goats are the most numerous livestock in the USSR and number 145 million (USA 17 million); there are 71 million pigs (USA 68 million) and 102 million cattle (USA 115 million), of which 41 million are cows (USA 12 million).

There are three types of farm in the Soviet Union: state farms, collective farms and private plots. There are some 12,000 state farms and they are of enormous size—an average of 60,000 acres. The land is owned by the state and the farms are run by managers put in by the Ministry of Agriculture; they are found mainly in areas recently ploughed up, as in the dry steppe of northern Kazakhstan. Collective farms, which number 36,000, are also very large, having an average size of 15,000 acres: here the land, although owned by the state, is held in perpetuity by the farmers, who elect a chairman to direct the operations. A fixed quota of produce has to be delivered to the state and the remainder is either shared out among the members or sold in urban markets or to industrial enterprises. Any profit resulting from sales to the state and elsewhere is also shared between the members, but these now have a guaranteed minimum wage. The private plots are very small and only about an acre in size, but there are nearly 15 million of them and they produce 13 per cent by value of farm production: normally there is one for every collective farm household.

The farm population numbers 48 million or 20 per cent of the total, and at harvest time this number is swollen by reinforcements from the towns, colleges and the army. Over half the farm workers are women, and because so many young people have left the farms, about a quarter of the labour force is made up of old age pensioners.

By American standards the capital equipment of Soviet farms is inadequate. They have at their disposal well below half the number of tractors and trucks available to American farmers, and fewer combine harvesters. The standard of maintenance is

Passengers waiting in the snow of a dark December day for an electric train to take them into Moscow from a station out in the country.

In rural districts horse and sledge are still the main means of private transport in winter. In the background is the traditional *izba* or Russian log house.

low and much machinery is idle for lack of repair facilities. A few years ago little fertiliser was used on Soviet farms, but since 1960 there has been a sharp rise in output to well above the American level. But fertiliser in the Soviet Union is not graded and packed to American standards: farms have little say in when they will receive it, how much they will get and of what kind. Owing to lack of storage facilities there is considerable wastage from exposure to the weather.

FISHERIES AND FURS

The Soviet fish catch has grown with amazing rapidity. Between 1950 and 1960 it doubled from 1,755,000 to 3,541,000 metric tons, and between 1960 and 1970 it doubled again to about 7 million tons. This compares with an American catch of 2 million tons and a British figure of just over 1 million tons. Only Peru and Japan now catch more fish than Russia. This dramatic expansion of Soviet fishing is a result of government investment in modern trawlers and factory ships. The more modern factory vessels in the Russian fishing fleet are able to can 50 tons of fish, freeze a 100 tons and manufacture 120 tons of meal daily while

---

Chess enjoys remarkable popularity amongst all classes of society and few games are without their eager onlookers. This one is being played in the Kirov Park in Leningrad.

Muscovites can seek respite from the oppressive summer heat at several bathing places in and around the capital, as at this popular one in Sokolniki Park, which is equipped with benches and sun shelters.

at sea. The trawler fleet is being re-equipped with new re-frigerated diesel-electric vessels. The private companies and fishermen of other nations find it difficult to compete with state-aided application of modern technology on such a scale.

In her vast northern forests the Soviet Union has an unrivalled variety of fur-bearing animals, and although these continue to be trapped, the growth of fur-farming has reduced the importance of naturally bred furs. The export of furs earns Russia some 80 million roubles a year.

FORESTRY

Although the immense Soviet forests give the USSR by far the largest timber resource in the world, much of it is in remote and inaccessible places. Russia west of the Urals uses more than half the Soviet output of timber, but well over 80 per cent of this output comes from Siberia. Consequently it has to be transported over immense distances. Not only is there a massive movement from east to west, but also from the forested north to the very largely treeless south. The rivers take a big share of such movement and a common sight on the Volga are the immense rafts of timber guided by motor vessels fore and aft.

Lumbering is the chief occupation of the forests of northern Russia and is found along the waterways and railways and close to the power stations. The industry has been modernised and the axe, handsaw and horse have given way to electric saws, powered cranes and diesel tractors. Diesel trailers bring the logs, 500 at a time, in to vast timber yards which occupy clearings in the forest; here they are sorted out and stacked before making their way to river, canal or railway for transport to the sawmills. The lumberjacks now live in permanent villages of wooden cottages erected in the forest near the central timber yards, a great improvement on the temporary shacks in which they were formerly housed. Close by the sawmills are to be found the various wood-processing industries—making matches, plywood and veneers, furniture and prefabricated parts for houses—and also the wood chemicals industry. This produces wood alcohol, glucose and other products from waste material derived from the sawmills, and manufactures pulp and paper from timber not fit for lumber.

TRADE UNIONS

The trade union movement in Russia is one of the more admirable parts of the Soviet system. Trade unions are guaranteed immunity from outside interference by law, although, inevitably, Communist Party members play a leading part in their activities. Their officials are elected by secret ballot among the members. They do not act as militant organisations to fight management for more pay, nor do they call strikes. Instead they act as guardians of the workers' rights and welfare. Their consent is necessary for changes in wage structure and rates and for the disposal of funds set aside for bonuses and incentive schemes. If they consider it advisable they can send a worker off to a rest home and arrange leave of absence on compassionate grounds. Their consent is necessary before any worker can be dismissed. The Soviet trade union movement has legislative initiative—ie it has the power to draft legislation in the workers' interest and bring it before the Supreme Soviet.

Although the trade union officials normally co-operate with management they have important legal powers to overrule it if they find it necessary. As an extreme measure they can close down a factory. This happened, for example, in the Gulyaipole agricultural machinery works in the Ukraine in 1971. The ministry responsible responded to repeated protests about working conditions with nothing more than promises. In the words of a trade union official, 'In the case of these two shops we could no longer put up with the delay in solving the serious safety problems there. And so, the union was compelled to close them down.' As the two workshops in question were vital to production, the whole factory was forced to close. The ministry soon acted to have the measures demanded by the union put in hand.

PLANNING

At the top of any Soviet industry comes the ministry, which is divided into departments. For example, the Ministry of Food Production has departments for Bread, Confectionery, Salt, Sugar, Vegetable Oil, Wine and many other commodities. Below the departments are *oblast* combines, which are responsible for the enterprises of the department within a county or *oblast*. Thus the Kursk Sugar Combine controls all the sugar refineries in Kursk *oblast* in central Russia. The method of planning production and the input of resources are complex and cumbersome. Every August each individual sugar refinery will produce its plan for the coming year, stating what it plans to achieve and what it needs to achieve it. The Kursk *oblast* Sugar Combine modifies this in accordance with its own regional policy. It then goes on to the Department of Sugar Production where it may again be altered, and finally to the Ministry of Food Production where it is co-ordinated with the plans of the other departments. The ministry does not have the last word, as its programme may now be modified by the State Planning Commission (Gosplan) as part of the national plan.

The annual plan, thus pieced together from data that have come upwards through the administrative system, now descends again by way of department and combine to the individual enterprise. At each stage responsibility, targets, input and output requirements are subdivided: among the many departments at ministerial level, among the combines at departmental level, and among the factories at combine level. When the factory finally gets its own plan back it may be unrecognisable from the one it sent in.

During the 1960s modifications to the system which allow much greater scope to the individual factory management were cautiously introduced. Instead of the plan, as finally received, specifying everything in great detail, it now confines itself more to overall targets and to more general guide lines, and leaves more to the initiative of the manager of the enterprise. He has greater freedom to choose his materials and his suppliers, to introduce modifications or technical innovations, to set prices and to make profits. Furthermore, the factory has considerable discretion as to how to spend any profits it may make above the 10 per cent it must return to the state. Such moneys can be redistributed to the workers as bonuses, or used to build or improve clubs, canteens and other facilities, and even to erect housing for the employees. These changes are known as the new economic reform in the Soviet Union, but abroad they are often termed the 'Liberman reforms' as they were first advocated by a Russian economist of that name. In practice many enterprises have proved to be too small to take advantage of the reforms. Consequently the 1971–5 five-year plan is witnessing a campaign for the amalgamation of small firms into larger units.

The complicated bureaucratic machinery can be frustratingly slow moving, and it is particularly weak in providing the kind of everyday communication between managers of enterprises which, though coming under different ministries, need constant contact with each other. To remedy this a class of unofficial intermediaries has come into being. These are known as *tolkachi* and they somewhat resemble the commercial travellers of the capitalist world. They get to know so much about the needs of an industry—where supplies can be had, which are of good quality and which poor, where surplus stock can be most profitably disposed of, that their services are invaluable to managers, who pay them out of the enterprise's funds.

During the course of the 1971–5 five-year plan the organisation of the Soviet economy is being transformed by the introduction of a computerised system and the application of economic-mathematical methods. Although Russia has lagged behind the Western world in the use of computers, she will be the first country to use them for the direction of the national economy.

MANAGEMENT

Soviet managers differ in background from those of the Western world. They are almost always university graduates in engineering. They fully understand the technical and production aspects of their work, but know little of finance and marketing, which are so important to the capitalist manager. The Russian manager works under great pressure to achieve his production target, yet he is mercilessly exposed to many watchful eyes. State officials can at any time investigate any aspect of his factory's work; trade union officials can insist that he keeps on some difficult or fractious worker; such a worker can write a letter attacking him to the newspaper and it will probably be published; active Party workers may call him to account for complaints they have received from dissatisfied customers. If he succeeds he will earn handsome bonuses, but if he fails he will lose his job. To succeed he must keep the goodwill of the many officials in a position to criticise and ruin him. This he may be able to do since most of them are, like him, interested in convincing their superiors that everything that they are responsible for is going well. Keen to fulfil the plan and earn his bonuses he may be tempted to misappropriate the funds at his disposal—perhaps to raid the workers' welfare fund in order to buy machinery that will increase his output.

POLLUTION

In all advanced countries, industrialisation has led to serious and extensive pollution of the environment. Awareness of and concern for this problem are widespread in the USSR and most local soviets have now set up 'committees for nature protection' whose job is to watch for the harmful effects of pollution. These committees recommend to the soviets bylaws which, if accepted, give the force of law to restraints upon offending enterprises.

Such measures have involved the petrochemical industry in the expenditure of millions of roubles on remedial measures.

FOREIGN TRADE

After the Revolution the Soviets resolved upon a policy of economic self-sufficiency. The dependence of tsarist Russia upon foreign imports had enabled the German blockade to bring the country to defeat, and Stalin was determined that this should not happen again. The country must live on what it could produce, however great the sacrifice imposed upon the population. In consequence Soviet foreign trade was minimal until the 1950s. It has increased greatly since then because, with the discovery and exploitation of the country's immense wealth in natural resources, large surpluses of such commodities as timber, coal, oil, gas, iron and other metals have become available for export. This has financed greater imports: these do not weaken the self-sufficiency of the state because the Soviet Union has developed all branches of its economy beyond the point at which it could be successfully blockaded. But foreign imports of machinery and machine tools, and in some cases of whole factories, do enable the rate of industrialisation to be speeded up, while imports of food and consumer goods make possible the raising of the standard of living of the people. At one time Soviet trade was hampered by the long list of 'strategic goods' which the United States would not allow countries dependent upon it to send to Russia. But as the countries of western Europe and Japan recovered from the 1939–45 war and became increasingly independent, they were tempted by the prospect of trade with Russia to persuade the USA to narrow the list or to defy the embargo. In 1972 the United States, having long denied itself a significant share in Soviet trade, made drastic reductions in the list of prohibited exports.

Soviet trade, which was valued at only 3 million roubles in 1950, had risen to 10 million by 1960 and to over 20 million in 1970. It still, however, amounts to little more than a quarter of the American total, and is only about two-thirds of British trade. Although most Soviet trade is with other socialist countries— the countries of eastern Europe are its leading commercial partners—trade with the capitalist world is growing markedly. In 1950 it was only 19 per cent but by 1958 it was 26 per cent and is now over 35 per cent of the total. Japan and West Germany are the leading capitalist countries in trade with Russia, but Britain, France and Italy are also important. Britain, a few years back, did more trade with Russia than any other non-communist country, but this has declined sharply since 1970. Most of her competitors have gone to some lengths to avoid worsening their relationship with the Soviet Union, since it offers an immense potential market for goods of all kinds, if its leaders are to fulfil their promise of a rapidly rising standard of living.

Political factors are very important in Russian commerce. Trade with France rose rapidly after President de Gaulle made his accord with the USSR. Trade with West Germany has increased strongly since Chancellor Brandt embarked on his *Ostpolitik*. China and Cuba offer remarkable instances of the importance of international politics in Soviet trade. In 1960 China occupied second place among countries trading with the USSR and their mutual commerce was valued at $1\frac{1}{2}$ billion roubles. By the end of the decade China had fallen to thirty-sixth in rank and Sino-Soviet trade had declined to a mere 50 million roubles. In 1958 Soviet trade with Cuba was negligible, but the island is now Russia's most important trading partner outside of Europe. American embargo and Soviet friendship determine the direction and nature of Cuba's trade. Although adjacent to rich oil-fields, her petroleum is brought thousands of miles from Russia; although close to the world's largest sugar-consuming and sugar-importing nation, her sugar surplus is carried away to the distant Soviet Union, a country self-sufficient in sugar.

Soviet exports and imports balance approximately in value, but not by weight. Exports, which consist mainly of bulky primary commodities, outweigh imports nearly ten times. Fuels, ores, concentrates and metals make up about 40 per cent of

Soviet exports and go to forty different countries. Italy is the chief importer of Soviet petroleum, followed by Czechoslovakia, East Germany, Poland, Bulgaria, West Germany and Finland. Over 20 per cent of Soviet exports consist of machinery and industrial and transport equipment: this goes to eastern Europe and also to many of the 'developing' countries in the form of aid.

On the import side machinery and industrial and transport equipment form the leading category, amounting to nearly 40 per cent by value. These goods come mainly from the more highly industrialised countries of eastern Europe, especially East Germany, from the more advanced countries of western Europe and from Japan. They are followed in importance by consumer goods and foodstuffs, which together account for over 30 per cent of Soviet imports.

Much Soviet trade results from bilateral, barter-type agreements such as that made with West Germany in 1970 to exchange natural gas for steel pipe.

6

How They Learn

THE communist leaders of the Soviet Union regard education as the means by which a superior type of man will be produced—Soviet man, imbued with the philosophy of Marx and Lenin and idealistically and unselfishly ready to build and maintain a communist society. Education is not looked upon, therefore, merely as a means of passing on knowledge and training the mind, but as an essential creative process. Its purpose is not just academic. It is also economic—to train better workers; social—to produce good citizens; cultural—to foster a lively interest in the arts; political—to turn out men and women willing and able to operate a socialist system; and patriotic—to induce a love of the motherland and a determination to defend it at all costs.

The best way of achieving all these aims is thought to be through the teaching of the Marxist-Leninist philosophy from which the ideals of communism stem, for this philosophy gives—in the belief of the country's rulers—a correct and unified interpretation of these same aspects of life: the economic, social, cultural and political. This philosophy permeates the whole educational system from nursery school to university. In nurseries and kindergartens little children learn to regard Lenin as a father who is solicitous for their welfare and from whom all good things come, and henceforth his picture will look down upon them wherever they are. In the upper forms of secondary schools and all institutions of higher education, Marxist-Leninist philosophy is formally taught—as social studies—and a pass is required in this subject before a university student may graduate. There seems to be resentment among many students and their teachers because of the time they are compelled to give to this course.

GENERAL AND SPECIAL EDUCATION

Education in Russia is divided into general and special. The general education is that provided for the great majority of the country's children—the 50 million who go to the 200,000 general schools of the country. Special education, in which there is a bias in favour of one or more academic, professional or technical subjects, is of two grades, intermediate and higher. At intermediate grade it caters for about 4½ million boys and girls of secondary school age, and at the higher grade for another 4½ million students in colleges and universities.

SOVIET SCHOOLS

Of the 50 million pupils in general schools, 21 million are in the primary grades 1–4 (ages 7–10); 21 million in the junior secondary grades 5–8 (ages 11–15), and nearly 8 million in the secondary grades 9–10 (ages 16–17). A ten-year schooling period has now been introduced universally, so that in future every child will attend school until he is 17.

Every nationality in the country important enough to form a separate administrative division, from Union Republic down to national district, uses its own language in its schools. As a result education is carried on in 53 different languages, in each of which a full range of text books has to be provided. This is an immense task when it is considered that some 300 million copies of about 2,600 different text books are published each year.

The school year begins on 1 September and continues for nine months, giving a long summer holiday of three months. Every year about 9 million children attend one of the Young Pioneers (Boy Scout/Girl Guide) camps during this period. Children aged 7–10+ are at school for 24 hours a week. Those aged 11–17 for 30 hours a week. Where the language of instruction is not Russian, these times are increased to allow for the study of Russian. Schools are generally co-educational.

Standards are maintained by teams of inspectors and merit is rewarded with certificates and, for exceptional brilliance, with gold and silver medals. Now that secondary education to 17 for all has been introduced, every child will take the examinations for the State Certificate of Secondary Education before he leaves. There is an end-of-year exam in every grade, and those who fail have to stay down for a second year in the same class. The maximum size of class is fixed at 40 for grades 1–8 and at 35 for grades 9 and 10.

A serious attempt is being made to improve Soviet education by placing less emphasis on factual content and more on thought processes and reasoning. This has involved rewriting text books, and the USSR Minister of Education, Mikhail Prokofiev has said:

> *The new text books, compiled by prominent scientists in connection with method-teachers, are more succinct in their facts and more widely embracing in their analysis of natural laws . . .*
>
> *The changeover is by no means automatic or easy or even to the liking of all teachers, pupils and parents. It is much more complex; the course we have chosen is more like a country road full of pitfalls than a modern highway. Our experience shows that many authors of text books are having trouble in eliminating excessive factual material and discarding secondary facts, which they often regard as of prime importance. Hence the voluminousness of some of our books. Teachers not only have to master the new material—this is relatively easy; they have to work out the best ways of putting it across in class. A great deal of time and energy is being swallowed up in regearing.*

The schools have a teaching staff of 2,600,000, 90 per cent of whom are graduates or trained in an institute of education or a training college. Women form 71 per cent of them, and in primary schools the proportion rises to 87 per cent. Modern schools are usually low spacious buildings of only one or two storeys, but many old multi-storey buildings are still in use. Some of them are overcrowded and have to work on a shift system. Most schools take pupils for the whole ten-year period from grade 1–10, and many urban schools have well over a thousand pupils.

Soviet educational establishments are not nearly so regimented from above nor as standardised in matters of administration and curriculum as one might expect and there is a surprising opportunity to experiment. Most of the reforms that have been introduced in recent years have come from the work of individual teachers experimenting in their schools. In a few schools the staff choose the headmaster, and in some schools in Georgia marks have been abolished.

TELEVISION

In recent years, as in the West, emphasis has been placed on school television, programmed instruction and teaching machines. School television began in Moscow in 1970, and now each Republic has its own service. The educational channel is called the Third Programme and it puts on material suitable for kindergarten, primary school, secondary school, university students, correspondence course students, and various professional and vocational groups. About 700 of Moscow's 1,000 schools can receive the programmes. In the 1969–70 school year the following courses were given: second-year nature study, fifth-year geography and music, 5th- to ninth-year history and literature, sixth-year physics, seventh-year chemistry, eighth-year physics, and tenth-year biology, chemistry and social studies.

The following extract from an article on the subject by Campbell Creighton in the *Anglo-Soviet Journal* (September 1970) gives some detailed illustration of topics dealt with:

A lesson on Grieg and another on the classical Greek theatre (history) for the fifth class; Chekhov's Chameleon, *and Magellan and the voyages of discovery for the sixth class; egg-laying and marsupial mammals, and primates [seventh-class zoology], the physics of radio transmission and reception [for the eighth class] ; Lenin's GOELRO Plan [ninth-class history] ; the synthesis of protein [tenth-class chemistry] ; and mytosis [tenth-class biology]. Various approaches are used. The fifth-class lesson on the classical Greek theatre used excerpts from Moscow theatre productions of plays by Sophocles, Aeschylus, Euripides and Aristophanes. A lesson on the feudal castle took the form of the adventure of a sixth class schoolboy who was suddenly dropped into the Middle Ages with no more knowledge about it than he had gleaned from the school history book. And a lesson on the Arab Caliphate was presented in the form of a story about the small son of the Caliph on a journey through his father's realm.*

KINDERGARTENS

Many children attend nursery schools at the age of 3 and most go to kindergarten for one or two years before starting school at 7+. They spend 14 hours a week in kindergarten. Of these 4 hours go to familiarising the infants with their environment and their native language, and preparing them for reading and writing, 2 hours to elementary mathematics, 2 hours each to drawing, music and physical exercises, 1 hour to modelling and 1 hour to cutting, pasting or constructing. The first lesson lasts 35 minutes, the others 20 or 25 minutes. There are almost 8 million children in nursery schools and kindergartens.

PRIMARY EDUCATION

Two notable reforms were introduced into Soviet education in the 1960s on an experimental basis and have now become universal. The first was the condensing of the primary school period from four years to three, ie from grades 1–4 to grades 1–3 inclusive.

In 1957 Professor L. Zankov, convinced that speedier methods could be used in teaching reading, writing and arithmetic, undertook research the results of which supported this belief. In 1962 his methods were tried out in thirty classes, and their use was cautiously but steadily expanded as success became evident. Primary school education became much less didactic and there was much less learning by heart. The school year 1971–2 saw the application of the 3 year primary course to the whole of the USSR. As a result of this reform another year has become available for secondary education, making it possible to drop the eleventh grade and to achieve a universal 10 year schooling period.

The second successful reform was the introduction of algebra and other mathematical techniques, previously delayed until the secondary stage, at the beginning of the primary course. Elementary algebra is now taught in all Soviet primary schools, and even the rudiments of set theory—formerly only taught in higher educational establishments—have been experimentally introduced in some.

In grade 1 the 24 hour week devotes 12 hours to reading and writing the native language, 6 to mathematics, 1 each to art and music, and 2 each to physical education and practical work. In grades 2 and 3 there are 2 hours fewer for the language and these are spent on nature study.

SECONDARY EDUCATION

At the secondary stage education is 'general' for the vast majority, and 'special' for the few who show exceptional talent in one direction. These latter go to schools which, while still offering a general education, make possible much more rapid progress in the subject specialised in. There is also a variety of vocational secondary schools, where pupils may spend the final one, two or three years of the secondary school period. Until recently the general secondary schools allowed no optional subjects. They are now being introduced, thereby increasing the flexibility of the system, but increasing the burden on the pupils as they are additional to rather than instead of existing subjects.

The school week at this stage has 30 hours of compulsory instruction to which 2 hours have been added for optional subjects in grade 7, 4 hours in grade 8 and 6 hours in grades 9 and 10. The time spent on the native language declines from 6 hours in grade 4 to none in grade 10, but literature maintains between 2 and 4 hours a week throughout. Mathematics has 5 or 6 hours, history 2 to 4 hours, biology 2 hours, a foreign language 2 to 4 hours, physical education 2 hours and practical work 2 hours. All these subjects are taught throughout the secondary period. Physics is introduced at grade 6 with 2 hours and rises to 5 hours in grade 10; chemistry comes in at grade 7 with 2 hours and rises to 3 hours in grades 9 and 10. Astronomy and social sciences are taught in grade 10 only, when they receive 1 and 2 hours respectively. Geography is taught in grades 5–9 (2 hours a week except in grade 6, when it is 3 hours); technical drawing is taught in grades 6–8 (1 hour a week). Art and music lose their 1 hour a week after grades 6 and 7 respectively.

The new secondary school curriculum summarised above incorporates changes introduced to use the extra time made available by abbreviating the primary course from 4 years to 3, and by extending the school-leaving age to 17. At the same time content has been drastically reformed to bring it closer to the reality of the modern world. There has been greater integration of mathematics with the natural sciences. Thus the physics course is based on molecular theory and the atomic structure of matter; it also includes the basic principles of relativity and the physics of the atomic nucleus. The introduction of the molecular-kinetic theory makes the chemistry more intelligible. Mathematics now includes calculus, co-ordinate geometry and computing techniques, which are essential to the modern study of natural science and engineering. Biology now encompasses ecology, physiology and evolution, and pupils study cell structure, genetics, heredity, selection and breeding. The options introduced with the new curriculum vary widely. Examples are geology, medicine, the history of art, motor-car engineering and agricultural machinery.

BOARDING SCHOOLS

More and more children are being sent to boarding schools for various reasons: because they are orphans, because their parents dwell in remote areas inaccessible to schools or live a semi-nomadic life, or because some factor in their home life makes it desirable. There are also health schools established in salubrious areas for children who need a special environment for convalescence or other medical reasons.

EXTENDED DAY SCHOOLS

Extended day schools, which provide care and education for children both of whose parents are working, have spread widely since they were introduced in 1964 and by the end of 1971 4 million boys and girls were attending them. These schools provide breakfast and a mid-day meal. The afternoon is spent in games and activities, and two hours in the evening are set aside for 'homework'. Teachers give the formal instruction during the long morning session and special tutors supervise the work and activities of the rest of the day. Training colleges are now giving special courses for tutors in extended day schools. Parents contribute a small charge for meals.

EXTRA-CURRICULAR ACTIVITIES

Practical work, extra-curricular activities and aesthetic education are all regarded as most important, so much so that in 1967 it was decreed that each school should have a deputy head whose responsibility would be to look after these aspects. There is so much to do for the Soviet schoolchild that he has little time for boredom or mischief. All non-academic activities take place in his own time, not in lesson time. In a large urban school the

H

child will have a choice of very many games and sports: football, volleyball, basketball, athletics, boxing, table tennis, swimming and underwater sport, skating, ice hockey and skiing. He will be expected to belong to the Octoberites (something like the Wolf Cubs or Brownies) in the first two grades and to the Pioneers thereafter. At fourteen he will be eligible to join the Young Communist League (Komsomols). All these groups plan leisure activities in association with the school: often these are of a social character and may include weeding gardens or helping in the local kindergarten.

Most academic subjects have their clubs and there are societies or 'circles' for every conceivable interest, examples being spaceship modelling, go-kart racing, weaving and agronomy. An important feature of these activities is the way in which the whole community is drawn into their organisation. Whereas in Britain or America almost the whole burden would fall upon the staff of the school, in Russia many of those running the various societies are professional or amateur enthusiasts from outside; often these are parents. Likewise in the practical work hours of the curriculum, instruction is often given by technicians from neighbouring factories.

At present there is a drive to improve the relationship between the general school and industrial work, and arrangements have been made for pupils not only to visit factories but to work in them. In fact each general school is linked with some economic enterprise or other and the Party members do all they can to stimulate mutual co-operation and interest. In Moscow a special factory has been set aside where grade 10 schoolchildren do all the work, under qualified instructors. The factory, called *Chaika* (Seagull), has radio, printing, electrical, sewing and various other workshops and satisfactory performance in one of these earns the pupil a proficiency certificate. As for the specialised schools, those which deal primarily with technical subjects are attached to factories and, increasingly, built in as part of the factory or works.

HIGHER EDUCATION

There is a separate ministry for higher education. This is responsible for the 800 odd colleges and universities in the USSR. In these institutions of higher education about $2\frac{1}{2}$ million men and over 2 million women work for academic, professional and technical qualifications. This amounts to 190 per 10,000 of the population compared with 268 in the USA and 80 in the UK. There are 50 universities and numerous technical colleges, engineering institutes, agricultural institutes, medical colleges and colleges of education, etc. Higher education is expanding rapidly and 60 new institutions were opened in the course of the 1966–70 five-year plan, including 9 universities. Eight more colleges were added in 1971.

All higher education is free and students receive a monthly grant. These grants are barely enough and most students earn more by doing summer work; some go to farms, others join construction teams, many work as waiters and porters at hotels and resorts or act as guides for tourists, and many join various summer scientific expeditions, for working on which they are paid. Distinguished work in the end-of-year examinations can earn a 25 per cent increase of grant. The inadequacy of the existing grants was acknowledged by Brezhnev in October 1971 and grants were increased by 25 per cent from 1 September 1972. The new rates are 40–60 roubles a month for those in institutions of higher education and 30–45 roubles a month for those in specialised technical schools.

Students may choose their specialisation from 400 different subjects. The combined teaching staff of the higher education colleges is about 300,000, and 660,000 men and women took degrees in 1971. Of the nearly 5 million students in 1971, 20 per cent were in colleges of education and teachers' training colleges, and 11 per cent were studying economics, while most of the rest were in some aspect of engineering. Over 40 per cent of graduates were also in engineering and technical subjects.

UNIVERSITIES

Of the fifty-eight universities, the senior are those of Moscow (founded 1755), Tartu (1802), Kazan (1804), Kharkov (1805), Odessa (1807), Perm (1817), Leningrad (1819), Kiev (1834), Chernevtsy (1875), Tomsk (1898), Saratov (1909) and Rostov (1915). Vilnius, originally founded in 1579, was closed in 1832 and not reopened until 1919. Lvov was founded in 1661 but closed in 1805. It became part of the Soviet system in 1939. All the others have been opened since the Revolution.

The largest student enrolments are at Moscow (over 30,000) and at Leningrad (about 10,000). Although the universities are few in number compared with other institutions of higher education, their average enrolment—over 5,000—is much larger, and well over half of all students receiving higher education are in universities. Most of them live in hostels and pay only a very low rent—1 rouble a month. University students play an important part in university administration. There are faculty-student councils that advise on such matters as grants, entrance examinations, expulsions, etc. All lectures and classes are compulsory, but some faculty-student councils can recommend dispensation from this rule where the quality of a student's work is high enough.

Moscow University is by far the largest. It has 13 faculties made up of 214 chairs, 4 research institutes and many other ancillary institutions. A unique university is Lumumba People's Friendship University, which is exclusively for students from Africa, Asia and South America. It is named after Patrice Lumumba, a left-wing politician who was murdered while serving as the first elected prime minister of the Congo.

ADULT PART-TIME EDUCATION

Most of the institutions of higher education as well as the specialised secondary schools give evening classes and correspondence courses, and there are also a number of colleges that specialise in this type of work. The courses are often linked with current educational programmes on television and radio. Many large factories organise their own part-time training and educational courses. The Moscow Ball Bearing Works, for instance, runs about a hundred different classes, and attendance and success at these is the key to annual wage increases and to promotion. Workers undergoing industrial training or educational courses work a day less than the normal working week; they may not be put on night work, and are entitled to time off with pay to take examinations. Much adult education of a more cultural kind is provided by the trade unions, which also provide their members with libraries, lecture halls and theatres.

RESEARCH

The Academy of Sciences of the USSR and its various institutes are responsible for organising research, and each Republic also has its Academy of Sciences, which promotes research more specifically in those subjects of particular importance to its economy. During the 1960s the Academy of Sciences of the USSR set up a special complex of research establishments at a newly built centre called Akademgorodok near Novosibirsk in western Siberia. A similar research station is being built at Irkutsk in eastern Siberia. Universities and higher institutes are expanding their research facilities and students are being expected to do more research and to receive less instruction. One of the colleges that has introduced active research into the teaching process is the Moscow-Physico-Technical Institute where, after a thorough grounding in physics and mathematics in their first years, students move on to research. At the Leningrad Institute of Technology senior students, after their basic course work, go on to the research departments of industrial enterprises in the city. Almost every large factory or works now has its research department.

In 1967 the 'scientific production centre' was introduced to solve the problem of securing the practical application of scientific discoveries. These centres are research organisations to which factories are attached in which new inventions or developments can be tried out.

7

How They Travel and Move
Their Goods

ALL major forms of transport in the USSR are public. There is, however, no single Ministry of Transport, but there are separate ministries for rail, inland waterways, sea and air transport. Road transport has no national direction and the various fleets of lorries belong to individual industries, to municipalities and to collective farms. Recently, however, an organisation called *Sovtransavto* (Soviet Motor Transport) was set up to run freight and passenger services by road to European countries. The absence of a single overall authority means that there is less co-ordination of transport than one would expect in a socialist economy.

Unlike Western countries there is little passenger travel by private car and most of what there is takes place in and around the towns. Inter-city passenger movement by car is almost non-existent. Thus, whereas in the United States nearly 90 per cent of all passenger miles travelled are by car and less than 1 per cent by rail, in Russia over 60 per cent are by rail and less than 0·1 per cent by car. The bus is also more important in the Soviet Union and accounts for 14 per cent of passenger movement compared with only 2 per cent in America. But air transport occupies second place in both countries, making up 21 per cent of passenger turnover in Russia and 9 per cent in America. In this respect the two superpowers are far ahead of any other country.

In the inter-city movement of freight the railway is again preponderant, accounting in 1971 for 82 per cent of the total turnover. Pipelines were next in importance with 10 per cent, followed by inland waterways with 6 per cent and motor transport with only 2 per cent. If, however, all transport of freight is taken into account, including movement on and off the farms, then the share of rail falls to 75 per cent and that of motor transport rises to 7 per cent, since almost all farm transport is by lorry/truck.

RAILWAYS

The reasons for the overwhelming predominance of the railways are several. The geography of the country with its slight gradients over most of the populated area favours railways, while the hard winter frosts break up roads. Geology has also militated against roads by covering the surface with light sands and clays so that road metal is difficult to find. As a result, the Soviets inherited from tsarist Russia a fairly well-developed rail system but only the sketchiest of road networks. Social and political factors are also important. In Western countries, where most people own cars, there is strong pressure for more and better roads and a readiness to pay for them. The cost of making and maintaining them is spread over the whole population, and the road hauliers benefit, paying much less than their share, whether on a mileage or actual physical damage basis, and railways have been unable to fight against such unequal competition. In the USSR, with few roads and private cars, almost the whole cost of making and maintaining roads would fall upon the state. Soviet economists have worked out that the real cost of moving goods by motor transport is twenty-five times as high as moving them by rail, so there can be no question of the state choosing road transport, except for the shortest distances and for flexibility of distribution away from the railways.

Despite continued growth, the Russian rail route mileage remains modest compared with that of America and some European countries, when the small size of the latter is taken into account: USSR, 84,000 miles; USA, 208,000 miles; countries of the original EEC together with the UK, 74,000 miles. The 1971–5 plan provides for the construction of another 3,500 miles. Most of the new lines will be branches from the main trunk routes to areas hitherto remote from railways. The remarkable fact is, that a route length well below half the American supports a passenger and freight turnover equal to that borne by the rest of the world's railways put together. Passenger turnover in 1970 was 145 billion passenger-miles, and freight turnover in 1971 was 1,645 billion ton-miles, and both totals are expected to increase by about a quarter by 1975. Such high figures can only be achieved by speedy turn-around times (a third of the American) and the most intensive use of the track, and this is made possible by the high degree of electrification: by 1975 25,000 miles—nearly a third of the total route length—will have been electrified.

Because the railways work to full capacity round the clock, the costs of operating them per passenger or per ton of goods are exceedingly small. This is reflected in the low fares for passengers: $1\frac{1}{2}$ kopeks per mile is the standard rate but long-distance trains, which are composed wholly of four-berth sleepers, are dearer, though still inexpensive compared with other countries; $3\frac{1}{2}$ kopeks a mile second class and 4 kopeks a mile first class. Children under 5 travel free; those aged 5–10 pay a quarter fare; from the age of 10 until they cease full-time education young people pay half fare between 1 October and 15 May. A variety of excursions and period tickets at reduced rates are available. The Soviet railways must be unique in having only reduced their fares during the past 25 years.

Another result of intensive use is that the system makes immense profits. Even after 3 billion roubles have been handed over annually to the state, there is enough left for the continual expansion, improvement and modernisation of the system. Under the 1971–5 plan the railways will get 430,000 new freight cars compared with 258,000 under the 1966–70 plan, and automatic block signalling or central train control will be introduced on 15,000 route miles. Automation will take over in 35 marshalling yards in addition to the 65 already automated. Soviet railways are being equipped to handle more and more container traffic and are increasingly used by Japanese exporters to Europe, who find that sending goods in containers across the Eurasian 'land bridge' saves 20 per cent over the cost of the sea route.

Because of the density of traffic on the lines it is not possible for Soviet passenger trains to reach very high speeds, nor are such speeds part of the future programme as they are on some European railways running far fewer trains. The Moscow-Leningrad line is an exception, however, and new multiple-unit rolling stock introduced in 1972 has a top speed of 125mph. Lines serving holiday resorts, which are relatively free of heavy goods traffic, also have faster trains which run at 60mph.

The two classes on Soviet trains are 'soft' or first and 'hard' or second. These terms date from the time when some carriages were upholstered while others were bare wood. The plain wooden cars are gradually being eliminated. The 'hard' class now has padded and covered seats or berths, while the 'soft' class has more spacious and softer spring-cushioned seats or berths. On ordinary trains the standard coaches have a central corridor with seats on both sides and a washroom at each end. They are watched over by an attendant, usually female. There is normally a buffet car.

Travel on Soviet railways is full of human interest, if only because of the widely differing backgrounds and ethnic or national origins of the passengers. The travellers are soon in vivacious conversation and, after a while, some will open up their string bags or newspaper-wrapped parcels and bring forth a variety of food and drink. The cases and bags that make up baggage elsewhere are seldom carried by ordinary working-class passengers.

On long-distance trains like the Trans-Siberian, which travels the 5,000 miles from Moscow to Vladivostok in seven days, four-berth compartments offer plenty of room and comfort during the day, seating only two aside, with a table between which can be used for meals or chess. At night the two seats become the lower berths while above them are the two upper berths. As passengers are allocated to these compartments irrespective of sex, the necessary dressing and undressing without benefit of curtains can be embarrassing to the bashful, which may be why many passengers travel in pyjama suits. The lavatories at either end, often out of order or locked by the attendant for reasons difficult to discover, are inadequate; for the coaches, like all forms of Soviet transport, are always full to capacity. Each coach has two attendants who bring the passengers' tea and biscuits at frequent intervals, exercise the watchful care expected of all Soviet officials over their charges, and spend the rest of the time busily sweeping, scrubbing, polishing and cleaning. Passengers in the 'soft' class will include army officers, old age pensioners visiting sons and daughters who have left their home district to live in a distant part of the Soviet Union, young engineers, and young geologists and others involved in the economic development of the nation, on their way to or returning from an assignment in Siberia. In the 'hard' class will be mainly young workers and their families, and soldiers.

MOTOR TRANSPORT

The relative scarcity of roads in the USSR has inhibited the development of motor transport and much of what there is does not take place on roads as it does almost wholly in Western countries, but on farm tracks, on desert trails, and in winter, on the frozen rivers. The stock of vehicles is small by Western standards. The total of 3 million lorries/trucks—the United States has 18 million—is increasing slowly because production scarcely exceeds loss from the retirement of older vehicles. But when the great new truck plant on the Kama river comes into production the supply will greatly increase. As for private cars, there may be 3 million all told, compared with 90 million in the United States. A visitor to Moscow would find this hard to believe, because the wide streets are thronged with cars; but that is because a very large proportion of the Russian stock of automobiles is concentrated in the capital and, to a lesser extent, in some of the other larger towns. The enormous gulf in car ownership between Russia and the West is shown by the fact that whereas in 1971 Americans travelled an estimated 1,000 billion passenger miles by car or bus, for Russians the estimate was only 25 million —or 0·025 per cent of the American total. Buses are the normal means of reaching villages in the countryside. They usually begin their journeys at rail stations.

Khrushchev, when in power (1954–64), was implacably opposed to mass car ownership. After visiting America he said, 'We do not want such extravagance . . . We will develop public taxi pools . . . People will get their cars from them for necessary trips.' His successors reversed the policy and Kosygin is quoted as saying, 'You remember how the idea was propagated among us that our country did not need a large output of private cars. Everybody was expected to use buses. Everything was done to deny even managers of large enterprises and institutions the right to have a car. As a result, many of them had to use lorries.' But although steps have been taken to increase the production of cars, many difficulties will remain before the Russians have the same advantages in this respect as Westerners. Parking, garaging, service and repair facilities and fuelling stations are inadequate for the existing number of cars, and it seems unlikely that they will be expanded sufficiently to cope with the greater volume of traffic to come. Above all, the roads do not exist to make car ownership really worthwhile. Although there is an impressive length of unsurfaced tracks, surfaced roads total only about 120,000 miles compared with 3 million miles in the United States.

Almost all the cars used in Russia are of Soviet make and limited to a small range of models. There are the large *Chaika* limousines which seat seven, the *Volga*, which has been likened to the Swedish *Volvo* and seats five, and a small four-seater family saloon, the *Moskvich*. Most of the planned increase, already flowing from the large Fiat-built works at Tolyatti on the Volga, will consist of *Zhigulis*, named after the hills on the opposite bank of the great river. The little *Zhiguli* is meant to be the Volkswagen or 'people's car' of Russia. An improved and strengthened version of the Fiat 124, it is 13ft 3in long, 5ft 4in wide and 4ft 7in high. The fuel consumption is put at between 40 and 44mpg. Russian cars are on the dear side when related to income. A *Volga* costs about 5,000 roubles and there is a waiting list of several years. Russian cars are made without frills but they are sturdy and strong and stand up well to the rough conditions in which they often have to operate.

The contrast between the amount of freight moved by road in Russia and America, though not so glaring as it is for passengers, is none the less a strong one. In 1971 inter-city motor freight turnover in the Soviet Union was 47,400 million ton miles or about one-ninth of the American total. The chief reason is the much lower cost to the state of using and developing the intensively used rail system, but the nature of the Soviet economy is also a factor. The main requirement of the transport system has been hitherto to serve the basic industries. For this a skeletal network of main railway lines, enabling bulky goods to be moved to and from relatively few centres of heavy industry, has sufficed. But if the Soviet people are to have the promised utopia of abundant consumer goods, a further development of road transport will be essential. Factories making consumer goods need to be more widely dispersed than heavy industrial plant and the articles they produce could not be widely distributed among the population as a whole without an improvement in roads and an increase in road transport. Perhaps the giant new lorry/truck works at Chelniy-on-Kama is a sign that the Soviet leaders understand this.

Better rural roads are urgently needed. The chief single factor restricting Soviet agriculture is the short growing season, and every year much of the harvest is lost, either because it does not ripen, or, if it has ripened, because it cannot be gathered in before the onset of winter. Because surfaced roads are almost non-existent in the countryside, machinery and supplies cannot be brought to the fields, and farm work, therefore, cannot begin until the ground has dried out sufficiently to take heavy vehicles. At the other end of the season, as soon as the autumn rains come —the days being no longer long or warm enough for the moisture to be dried out, as happens in summer—vehicular use turns

the tracks into impassable quagmires. Any harvest not yet gar-
nered in must then be abandoned. An improved rural road
system would effectively lengthen the farm year at its beginning
and at its end.

INLAND WATERWAYS

With the coming of the railways in the second half of the nineteenth century the rivers of Russia lost their position as the chief
means of transporting goods, and their relative status has since
declined steadily. Winter freezing, spring flooding and shallow-
ness in summer and autumn were always drawbacks to their use.
Nevertheless, in absolute terms, they continue to handle more
and more traffic, their turnover of 115 million metric tons in
1971 being almost 60 per cent above the amount ten years
before, and four times as great as in 1951. About half the river-
and canal-borne freight is carried on the Volga-Kama system,
and the Soviet period has witnessed many improvements to this
great waterway. Canals have been cut linking it with Moscow,
with the Baltic Sea, and by way of the river Don with the Sea of
Azov and the Black Sea. The river Volga has been deepened and
widened in association with hydro-electric developments. Much
money has been invested in the provision of new shipping for the
carriage of both freight and of passengers. New 10,000 ton motor-
ships carry most of the cargo, apart from rafted timber, and
besides large and well-appointed passenger vessels, there are
speedy hydrofoils and hovercraft.

An interesting development has been the introduction of sea-
going vessels. These, built to the dimensions required by the
locks of the canals, are able to pick up cargoes on the banks of the
Volga or Kama rivers and deliver them overseas without the
necessity of trans-shipment at a seaport. Such ships, introduced
in 1965, have established maritime links between the interior of
Russia and nineteen foreign countries. They are able to navigate
from the Baltic Sea to the Black Sea across Russia without having
to round the peninsula of Europe.

Many rural areas without adequate roads are forced to depend on shallow streams and rivulets for their annual supply of bulky goods. These humble waterways, although they may be navigable for only a few weeks in spring, when swollen by rain and water from the melting snow, are essential to the rural economy. They are estimated to carry about 18 million tons a year, chiefly oil, fertilisers, farm machinery and foodstuffs, besides floating 300 million cubic feet of timber.

AIR TRANSPORT

Only the airways of the United States carry more cargo and passengers on their domestic routes than the Soviet airline *Aeroflot*. Air transport is peculiarly suited to such a large country with extensive areas difficult of access by surface means of transport, and the Soviets have taken full advantage of the opportunities offered. In many aspects of aircraft design the USSR leads the world, thanks largely to the work of Antonov, Ilyushin, Mikoyan, Tupolev and Yakovlev, the initial letters of whose names (AN, IL, MI, TU and YAK) appear on most aircraft in the service of *Aeroflot*. They are the Soviet equivalents of Boeing, Douglas, Lockheed and Martin in America. The supersonic TU-144, test-flown on 31 December 1968, has a maximum speed of 1,560mph, a range of 4,000 miles and a ceiling of 65,000ft. The Soviet Union is selling a growing number of its aeroplanes abroad. Besides conventional aircraft, helicopters are widely used and experimental work is being carried on with dirigible airships.

In 1969 the route length within the USSR was 362,500 miles and they carried 68 million passengers and 1,768 metric tons of cargo. In so doing they flew 44½ billion passenger miles and 1·22 billion ton miles, but even so their share of total freight turnover was less than 1 per cent. As in America they are far more important as carriers of passengers than of freight.

During recent years the comfort and service experienced on domestic flights have improved immeasurably over the days when there was no pressurisation. Seats are comfortable, food is good and hostesses attractive and attentive. When there are two compartments, children usually occupy the forward one. Fares are rather less than rail on shorter distances but higher on longer ones. Many people travelling by rail would travel by air if they could get seats, but planes are booked up for weeks ahead. Some sample single/one-way fares are given below (in roubles):

	Rail (*soft class*)	Rail (*hard class*)	Air
Moscow–Leningrad	16.00	13.90	13.00
Moscow–Kiev	19.20	16.40	15.00
Moscow–Novosibirsk	39.20	32.70	48.95

PIPELINES

Transport of oil and gas through pipes is the fastest growing form of transport in the Soviet Union, and second only to the railways. In 1950 the throughput of oil pipelines was 3 billion ton miles; in 1960 it was 32 billion, and in 1971, 200 billion ton miles. In addition, enormous quantities of gas are moved by pipe. Oil pipelines run from the Volga-Ural oilfield to the Moscow region, to the Baltic Sea, to the countries of eastern Europe and to the Far East. Gas pipelines from the Siberian, Central Asian, Ukrainian and North Caucasus fields bring gas to the Moscow region and export it across the frontier to both eastern and western European countries. Because the reserves are huge and the demand increasing, the latest pipelines to be laid are of exceptionally wide diameter—4ft—to obtain economies of scale, and larger diameters are planned for the future. In 1970 there were 44,000 miles of gas pipeline and in 1975 there will be 62,000. One hundred million people in the Soviet Union, or over 40 per cent of the population, have gas in their homes, and so rapid has been the growth of its use in industry that about 80 per cent of the country's steel, 60 per cent of its cement and 30 per cent of its electricity are produced in plants fuelled by natural gas.

ELECTRICAL TRANSMISSION

A rapidly increasing amount of the energy used in the Soviet Union is carried long distances by cable. Until recently the transmission of current over a thousand miles was not a practical proposition. But because so much of the Soviet Union's water power and coal lie in the eastern regions and energy is needed more and more in the west, there was a strong incentive for the Russians to overcome this drawback with technological advance, and this they have done. Super high-tension steel-aluminium cables using direct current are now being used to carry electricity for distances of up to 1,500 miles, and under the 1971–5 plan a 1½ million volt line is being built from a cluster of large new power stations on the Kazakh coalfield to central Russia, a distance of 1,800 miles.

SEA TRANSPORT

The Soviet merchant marine is growing fast and in 1971 had the sixth largest tonnage in the world and numbered 1,500 ships. In 1958 it was twelfth in world order. Amost 80 per cent of the vessels are less than ten years old and about a third are less than five years old. Just over half the Soviet trade by weight goes by sea, but the merchant fleet is also responsible for a considerable coastwise trade—ie the movement of cargoes and passengers from one Soviet coast to another. Most of this trade—about three-quarters—takes place on the Caspian, Black and Azov Seas, 15 per cent on the Pacific waters of the Far East, 5 per cent on the Baltic and 7 per cent on the northern sea route.

The northern sea route, in conjunction with the Baltic–White Sea canal, links Leningrad and the Baltic with the Arctic and Pacific coasts of the USSR. Despite its long hazardous course it is a much shorter sea route from the Baltic to the Pacific than the southern route which, with the Suez canal closed, necessitates sailing round the Cape of Good Hope and across the Indian Ocean. The Arctic coast of Russia began to be systematically navigated by cargo ships convoyed by icebreakers in 1935. During the 1941–5 war, when the Germans controlled the Baltic, the northern sea route was used to bring American goods along the Arctic coast and then up the various rivers. It is now used to carry supplies to the northern mining enterprises and, together with the great Siberian rivers, to deliver bulky freight to Siberian construction sites. Thus the generators for the world's largest hydro-electric power station at Krasnoyarsk, too large to travel by the Trans-Siberian Railway, were taken from Leningrad via the Baltic–White Sea canal, the northern sea route and the Yenisey river. The route is navigable for only four months of the year, and then only with the help of powerful icebreakers, like the nuclear-powered *Lenin*.

At a time when passenger travel by ship is in decline in the Western world, the Soviet Union has built an up-to-date fleet of passenger vessels already admired for their speed and comfort. Services are maintained between London and Le Havre and the various Baltic ports, between the ports of the Mediterranean and those of the Black Sea, and between the Soviet Pacific port of Nakhodka and Japan and Hong Kong. The *Alexander Pushkin* and the *Mikhail Lermontov* are the pride of the Russian passenger fleet. They maintain a transatlantic service to Montreal and Quebec in summer. These diesel-powered vessels each displace 19,000 tons, can carry 662 passengers with 1,500 tons of cargo, and sail at 20 knots.

URBAN TRANSPORT

At present most citizens of Soviet towns are wholly dependent upon public transport or their own legs, and trams/streetcars, trolley buses, omnibuses and taxis form a much larger proportion of the traffic than in the West; often the vehicles are old and decrepit and, during rush-hour periods, terribly overcrowded.

This is a result of housing the population in large and densely populated apartment blocks. When it is time to go to work these buildings pour forth such a multitude that even the most efficient public transport system—and that in Moscow is very efficient—cannot meet the demand.

The larger towns, including most of those whose population exceeds a million, have underground railway systems (subways) operating or building. These are clean and attractive; they are Soviet showpieces and great pride is taken in them. According to *Fortune* (February 1972) the Moscow underground carries more passengers a year (1½ billion) than any other in the world, though closely followed by the Tokyo (1·36 billion) and New York (1·30 billion) subways. Other Soviet towns with underground railways are Leningrad (370 million passengers a year), Kiev (100 million), Tbilisi (60 million), and Baku (40 million). Kharkov has one under construction, and they are being planned for Tashkent, Yerevan, Gorkiy and Kuybyshev. Fares are remarkably cheap. For 5 kopeks one can travel anywhere along the 86 miles of the Moscow Metro's lines and between any two of the 89 stations. Buses also have a single fare of 5 kopeks while for trolley buses it is 4 kopeks.

The 1971–5 plan envisages a much greater production of private cars than heretofore, and when the new factories at Tolyatti and Izhevsk, and the expanded plant at Moscow, reach their full output the effect is bound to be felt on the streets of Russian towns. Moscow already suffers from rush-hour congestion, and the accident rate is probably appalling. No general statistics are available, but some idea can be gained from a remark of the Chief of the State Traffic Control Department that, in 1968, 1,840 people were killed and 5,000 injured in Kazakhstan alone in motor accidents. If this casualty rate is applied to the whole population, the figures for the USSR would be 37,400 killed and 95,000 injured. Deaths in the United States, with 18 times as many vehicles, were 54,860 in 1968, and in Britain, with twice as many motor vehicles, 6,500. Pedestrians are the chief sufferers, and in the active discussion now being carried on in the Soviet press about the problems likely to accompany increased use of private cars, a favourite solution seems to be to discipline the pedestrian. The newspaper *Izvestya* writes with strange logic: 'Thousands of novices are going to take their places behind the steering wheel. Pedestrians, therefore, must be still more disciplined and penalties imposed upon them harsher.' And the weekly *Nedelya* complains that most accidents are due to the carelessness of pedestrians. No doubt journalists are among the new car owners. The traffic police also pounce upon pedestrians foolhardy enough to get in the way of a speeding truck while turning a blind eye to the latter.

The traffic police in the Soviet Union are a separate corps, distinct from the 'militia' or regular police, although they wear similar uniforms. They are known as the State Vehicle Inspection or from the initial letters in Russian, the GAI. They have the power to fine on the spot and can punch a hole in the motorist's log card; three holes bring suspension. Rigorous driving tests have been introduced and a great volume of propaganda for road safety put out in the schools and on television and radio. Driving has been made illegal after any consumption of alcohol. As a result of such measures sharp falls in the number of accidents were claimed for 1970 and 1971.

SPACE TRAVEL

More Russians have travelled in space than any other nation, and, unfortunately, some have perished as a result. Yuri Gagarin, on 12 April 1961, began the first manned space flight from the Soviet space research station at Baykonyr in Kazakhstan. Two years later Valentina Tereshkova became the first and only woman to travel in space, and 1971 saw the first orbiting space station (Salyut 1). In March 1965 Alexis Leonov was the first man to walk in space. No Russians have walked on the moon, a result of a policy decision made in the early 1960s that exploration of the surface of the moon and the planets should be automatic, on grounds that this was the safest, cheapest and most efficient means. Another reason for developing automatic probes was that, as conditions on some planets made manned landing extremely difficult if not impossible, the development of remotely controlled apparatus was essential. Successful stages in the Soviet investigation of the moon were the soft landing of Luna 9 in February 1966, the placing of the first moon satellite in orbit in April 1966 (Luna 10) and the return of Luna 16 with samples of moon rock in September 1970. In November 1970 an automatic moon car, controlled from earth—Lunokhod 1—was landed on the surface by Luna 17 and travelled between four and five miles during its three-month operational period. It bristled with instruments, many of French make, a result of Franco-Soviet scientific co-operation.

8

How They Play

SPORT, recreation and cultural activities are less spontaneous in Russia than in most countries. The state finances, encourages and controls all those forms of leisure-time pursuits of which it approves; and such activities are regarded as desirable, not so much for their own sake, but because they help to make a better citizen or a happier and healthier man. Participation in many sports and arts is also patronised because of the prestige that success brings to the Soviet state, and because it is government policy to promote international contacts through athletic and cultural activities. However, beneath this state-inspired and government-sponsored superstructure of serious and organised recreation lies the natural gaiety of the Russian people, which has, for centuries, expressed itself in song and dance and in many forms of convivial amusement.

SPORT

Since the war Soviet sport, with the help of a generous government sponsorship, has made immense progress. From a rather backward position among the nations the USSR now rivals the United States for world leadership. The Soviet peoples, although they turn out in tens of thousands to watch association football, ice hockey and other spectacles, filling immense stadiums, are participants rather than spectators. For many millions the day begins with physical exercises broadcast on the wireless; another 20 million have one or two 'keep fit' breaks of five minutes organised by the management or the trade union, at their office, factory or farm. Fifty-five million people regularly participate in the game and athletic activities run by sports clubs and sports centres. Most factories and farms have sports clubs and the sports centres are organised municipally for people who do not have access to clubs.

The National Games of the USSR involve most of those who take part in sport. They were first held in 1956 and again in 1959, since when they have been held every four years. In the 1956 competition there were 19 million entrants. A series of eliminating rounds are held locally and the finals, in which some 8,000 competitors take part, are held in Moscow. These games are on a bigger scale than the Olympics. During the Fourth National Games 46 national and 20 world records were broken and during the Fifth, 31 national and 18 world records.

The Soviet Union has 3,000 stadiums, 37,000 gymnasiums and 485,000 sports grounds, including 88,000 soccer pitches and 110,000 basketball courts. There are over 400 indoor swimming pools and numerous ice rinks and indoor arenas. Some of the stadiums are of large capacity. The Lenin Stadium in Moscow and the Kirov Stadium in Leningrad hold over 100 thousand spectators each. The immense cost of providing for Soviet sporting activities is financed by the state, by trade unions, and by the various offices, factories and farms which equip sports clubs. Membership of these costs the individual only 30 kopeks a year.

Of the various 'special' schools in the USSR, 142 specialise in training sportsmen. Many of the country's leading players and performers have jobs as instructors in such schools and in physical training colleges, or as trainers, coaches and referees. The most able sportsmen gain the title of Master of Sport, and those who take a distinguished part in international competitions, such as the Olympic Games, become Honoured Masters of Sport.

ATHLETICS

About 9 million people participate in track and field sports. Apart from the Olympic and National Games, the chief event of the Soviet athletic year is a visit of a team of American athletes. These superpower contests began in 1958, and the close rivalry which marks them is followed with keen interest throughout Russia.

VOLLEYBALL

This relatively new game has become the most popular participator sport in the USSR, holding the position occupied by tennis in many other countries. It has 7,200,000 players, over 2 million more than association football and 3 million more than basketball. The Soviet women's team won the world volleyball championship held in Sofia in 1970 and the 1972 Olympics. The men's team won the 1968 Olympics but came third in 1972.

ASSOCIATION FOOTBALL

Soccer is the leading spectator sport in the USSR and fills the great urban stadiums with enthusiastic crowds. As a participator sport it comes second with 4,800,000 players. Football is a summer game in the USSR and begins in April when the British season is coming to an end. Since 1958 the USSR team has always been among the top eight in world championships and among the top four in European championships. Individual clubs do not have such a good record and in the 1971–2 season only Moscow Dynamo survived the early rounds of the Cup Holder's Cup Tournament. However, the club reached the final.

In the internal championship recent years have seen the arrival of some new clubs in the front rank of Soviet football. Thus in 1971 the Soviet Championship was won by Kiev Dynamo (seventh in 1970) with Yerevan Ararat second (twelfth in 1970) and Tbilisi, third. In other words the first three places were held by Ukrainian, Armenian and Georgian clubs, and not as usual by Russians. The three 1970 leaders had been Moscow Spartak, Moscow Dynamo and Central Army. This is an indication of the way in which excellence at soccer is spreading throughout the Republics. A recent phenomenon has been the spread of six-a-side football, ascribed to the fact that it can be played at any season, indoors or out, and only requires a small pitch.

BASKETBALL

Basketball, with 4,200,000 players, is the third participator game in the USSR, and there are more basketball courts than football pitches. This popularity is the basis upon which Russia's prestige in the game has been built—she has won twice as many European championships as all the rest of Europe put together, and can compete with the United States and Brazil on equal terms. The Soviet Union came first in the 1972 Olympics.

ICE HOCKEY

Ice hockey is the Soviet Union's leading winter spectator sport, but it is not nearly so popular as a participator game, having only 550,000 participants. The annual international tournament held in Moscow is a highlight of the season, and top teams, like those from Canada, Sweden, Czechoslovakia and Poland, compete for the prize given by the newspaper *Izvestya*. The leading clubs are, in the main, those whose names are famous in soccer—Moscow Dynamo, Spartak, Central Army. The Soviet national team has won the world ice hockey title ten times, and nine times in succession.

Ice hockey played with a ball (bandy) is also popular in the USSR, and the Russians excel in this game, having held the world championship since 1957. Ordinary hockey played on grass was only introduced in 1969, but strenuous attempts are already being made to train a national team worthy of competing in the European tournament.

EQUESTRIAN SPORT

In 1934 the Soviet government began the breeding of thoroughbred racehorses, and brought three horses from England for the purpose. Thoroughbreds are now raised at many stud farms, the oldest and most famous of which is the Kabardinian, located on the North Caucasus steppe. The mating programme is supervised by the National Research Institute of Horse Breeding and by the Ministry of Agriculture. At the age of three thoroughbreds from the state stud farms are brought to the Central Hippodrome in Moscow to compete in the Grand Prix. In most large Soviet cities there are race courses, known as hippodromes, and despite the absence of gambling, horse racing is a popular sport, especially in the Republics of Central Asia. Other equestrian sports have also been raised to a high standard. A Russian horse and rider won the gold medal in the individual dressage event in the Mexico Olympics and the Soviet dressage team came first at Munich in 1972.

MOTOR SPORT

Motor sport scarcely exists in the USSR at the popular level because car ownership is so restricted and suitable roads so few, but the Russian car export agency has entered international rallies in recent years. In 1969 four Moskvich-412s entered the London to Sydney car marathon, and although only 56 of the 96 cars reached Sydney, all four Moskvichs did so. In 1970 three Moskvich-412s won third prize in the London to Mexico City World Cup rally. Only six of the twenty cars in their class completed the course. The Russian team included a Lithuanian taxi driver, a mechanical engineer from the State Automobile Research Institute, a test driver from the same institute and employees of the State Auto-Export Corporation. Motorcycle racing is a favourite sport with collective farmers and has long had organised competitions with prizes and cups for the successful. A popular new spectator sport is motoball, which is a kind of hockey played in the stadiums on motorcycles.

WATER SPORTS

Sailing, rowing and canoeing on the numerous lakes and rivers of the USSR have become popular forms of recreation in late years and reflect the rising standard of living. Russian yachtsmen won victories in the 1960, 1968 and 1972 Olympics but the sport of sailing is found in humbler form in much of the country, and collective farms organise their own regattas. As canoeists the Russians are second to none and they dominate the international championships.

WINTER SPORTS

All Russians learn to skate in infancy and many continue to do so well into adult life. The countryside abounds in natural skating rinks and, in the towns, areas in the parks are flooded and soon freeze over to make runs for races. There are also indoor skating rinks. In addition to amateur skating for recreation by the masses, there is much speed-skating, figure-skating and ice-dancing of a superb degree of finesse and these exhibitions of skill are watched by many thousands of spectators.

Although the Soviet Union has a long cold winter with plenty of snow, the land near the most densely populated areas is flat and offers only limited opportunities for tobogganing and skiing. However, it became customary in the eighteenth century to build artificial mounds for tobogganing and these were universally known as 'montagnes russes'. There are now towers of scaffolding constructed near Moscow and some other towns which provide artificial ski runs. For the Soviet amateur skier a holiday in the Caucasus Mountains is the event of the year, for the slopes of these mountains are ideal for the sport, and hotels, chair lifts and tow lifts have been built. One can now climb by cable to 12,000ft up the side of Mount Elbruz, whence some of the most daring runs in Europe are to be had.

OTHER GAMES AND SPORTS

Many other games and sports are played and enjoyed in the Soviet Union, and the number increases every year, although Rugby, American college football, baseball and cricket remain absent from the scene. Handball is one of several games that grew rapidly in popularity in the 1960s, and there are now regular city, Republic and All-USSR championships. Boxing, wrestling and weight-lifting are among the more strenuous sports in which Russia plays a leading role. At Munich in 1972 the USSR won eight gold and five silver Olympic medals in these sports, as well as two golds for fencing and one for judo. Boxing has been another late developer and the Russians did not make their international début until the 1952 Olympics. Many of the free-style wrestling champions came from Yakutia where wrestling has long been a national sport and a prominent activity at local festivals and celebrations. All the weight-lifting records are now held by Russians and the title of the 'world's strongest man' belongs to Vassily Alexeyev, who broke an Olympic record in 1972. Archery is another new sport in the USSR and Russian archers secured a bronze medal in the 1972 Olympics. Russian cyclists are to be found competing in the main European bicycling events.

The natural grace and agility of many Russians find expression in the degree of perfection that so many of them reach in gymnastics and callisthenics. The complete dedication to these exercises by both teachers and pupils, and the hours of exacting training they are willing to endure, astound the less fanatical devotees of these skills from other lands, and it is no wonder that the USSR normally carries off the Olympic gold medals. The Russian supremacy in the ballet is built upon the foundations of this natural passion for graceful and rhythmic body movement. Much the same zeal is shown in the development of the national love of song and dance. Russian groups of singers and dancers travel all over the world, winning universal applause and acclaim. They are but the finest exponents of arts that are widely diffused throughout the country, not only among the Russians, but also among many of the other peoples of the USSR, including the Koryaks from distant Kamchatka.

CHESS

The USSR is distinguished from all the leading nations of the world by the way in which the game of chess is played, regularly and seriously, by many millions drawn from all ranks of society. Nothing is more certain to be found in rest rooms of factories and collective farm clubs, in long-distance trains, and on park benches in summer, than this highly intellectual game. Its popularity may have originated in the need to while away long hours in the dreary winter time, and its present vogue may indicate the presence in the Russian character of an unusual degree of mental stamina, patience and intellectual concentration. It is not so much a private game as elsewhere, but a public spectacle. Whether played informally by farm or factory workers, or by grandmasters, there is sure to be an interested audience. Important matches fill large halls and the spectators who follow the moves on a large vertical board often have with them their own chessboards and sets on which they play out the game as it takes place. Chess is popular with women as well as with men.

It is not surprising that the USSR normally holds all the world titles and provides almost all the principal contenders. Although the appearance of the American Fischer at the top has disturbed this monopoly, he is only the third American to have reached the summit in world chess, whereas Russia has five men living who have held the world championship: Tahl, Smyslov, Botvinnik, Petrosyan (a Georgian) and Boris Spassky. Spassky's play in the 1972 world championship may have been affected by injuries sustained in a car crash.

CULTURE

Cultural activities in the USSR are expected to serve ideological ends. In the words of Yekaterina Furtseva, the Minister of Culture, 'Culture in the USSR is developing independently of anyone's financial gain and independently of commercial considerations. It is inspired, as Lenin predicted, not by considerations of profits but by the idea of socialism and feeling for the masses.' And certainly, if the number of people visiting art galleries and museums, going to the ballet and the theatre, and listening to concerts, is any guide the Soviets have succeeded in making culture truly popular and widespread among the masses. But although in no part of the world do the great masters of the past receive more homage, modern artists, composers and writers are expected to produce work consistent with the social and political ideals of the state and conducive to the advancement of these ideals.

The Communist Party's executive committee has complained that those who review works of art on television, radio or in the press often fail to apply the ideological touchstone to their criticism. Many reviewers, it was said,

> *show an inability to relate the phenomena of art to life. A conciliatory attitude towards works that are defective ideologically and artistically manifests itself . . . Criticism is still not active and consistent enough in asserting the revolutionary, humanist ideals of the art of socialist realism, in exposing the reactionary essence of bourgeois 'mass culture' and decadent trends, and in the struggle against various kinds of un-Marxist views on literature and art.*

As a result of such defects the Party called upon those concerned 'to raise the ideological and theoretical level of literary and art criticism and to see that it pursues the Party's line in the field of creative work in the arts in a more active way and with a principled approach'.

Because of such pressures most Soviet art still glorifies the historic deeds of the Revolution, the Great Patriotic War of 1941–5, and the industrial achievements of the workers in building a communist society. Soviet professional painters sell their work to the state, or to municipalities, trade unions, industrial enterprises and collective farms, all of which are expected to sponsor the arts by buying suitable works. Soviet writers likewise are dependent on state- or party-controlled publications for an outlet, unless they take the extreme step of allowing their work to be published abroad. That many artists and critics do not follow the Party line has been shown by some well-publicised incidents, such as the refusal to allow Solzhenitzyn to collect his Nobel prize and from such complaints as those voiced by the Party quoted above. Nevertheless, Soviet art— especially painting—has produced much impressive work with distinctive features, and no doubt what is lost through the subordination of art to ideology is balanced by the gain of having talent trained at state expense throughout all the classes and the many peoples of the Soviet Union.

Just as there are sports clubs and centres attached to enterprises and municipalities, so there are similar centres and 'circles' for cultural activities. In all there are some 300,000 such circles with over 4 million participators. Dramatic societies are the most numerous, there being over 73,000 of them with 850,000 participators, but the 70,000 choral societies have 1¾ million active members. There are besides, 45,000 choreographic societies (500,000 members) and 30,000 music societies (350,000 members).

BALLET

Ballet was introduced to the Russian imperial court in the eighteenth century during the reign of the Empress Anne (1730–40). While the art in Europe stagnated or declined, in Russia it seemed to graft naturally upon the national genius for the dance and flowered as never before. It reached perfection under the direction of Diaghilev at the beginning of the present century, and his famous company took the Russian ballet to the leading world capitals. Despite the interlude of a catastrophic period of revolution and war, the Bolshoy company of Moscow has maintained the international fame of the Russian ballet. Its success is underpinned by the intensive training and dedication to the art found in the many ballet schools throughout the country. These are united in the All-Union Conference of Choreography Schools, which holds annual contests from which the most gifted artists are selected for yet further training. The Bolshoy Ballet Company does not confine itself to the classics. In 1972 it gave the première of the first ballet to be made from Tolstoy's *Anna Karenina,* on which eight operas and thirteen films had been based, but no previous ballet. The very high production costs of such spectacles are partly met by state subsidies, enabling the price of tickets to be kept within reason, but because of this the theatres are always full and seats difficult to get. There are forty theatres for ballet and opera.

THEATRE

The live theatre flourishes in the USSR to an extent unparalleled elsewhere. This is in part because it is supported by the state, in part because of the interest in drama aroused amongst all classes at an early age by the children's theatres, and in part because there is less competitive entertainment than in the Western world. Actors are trained in special schools and, if they qualify, they are certain to find employment in one or other of the 500-odd professional companies. Although many plays are modern Soviet pieces with a strong ideological flavour, the great classics of prerevolutionary Russia and the Western world, notably Shakespeare, are often performed and prove extremely popular. Audiences are enthusiastic and listen and watch intently through programmes lasting sometimes for three or four hours. There are about 370 live theatres in the USSR where plays are performed professionally, and 110 million seats were sold in 1971.

The most remarkable aspect of the Soviet theatre is that children are catered for by special theatres where plays specially suited for young people are performed. There are nearly 150 such theatres and prices are relatively low—about 5⊙ kopeks a seat. The actors, who are mostly adult, receive the same pay as those working in the adult theatre. The children's theatres work in collaboration with the schools and their actors help with the running of school dramatic and debating societies. In 1965 children's opera was introduced to the children's theatre.

The puppet theatre is also popular in Russia, and the art reaches its most perfect form in the State Central Puppet Theatre in Moscow. This moved to a new specially designed building in 1971. It holds two auditoriums, one for adults and one for children, a puppet museum, and apparatus for a wide variety of lighting and sound effects. The large electronic clock outside the theatre is an introduction to the world of fantasy that awaits within. The clock, which is surmounted by a golden cockerel, has twelve little shuttered boxes from one of which an animal emerges to call out the time at every hour. At noon and midnight, all twelve animals appear and the clock chimes.

FILMS/MOVIES

Cinema-going continues to grow in the USSR despite the competing attraction of television. There are about 500 widescreen cinemas in the country, but films are also shown in the halls and lecture rooms belonging to various establishments, and about 160,000 film projectors are used for the showing of films to paying audiences. In all, about 4,700 million seats are sold annually, which means that, on an average, every inhabitant of the Soviet Union visits the cinema twenty times a year. Russians now go to see films five times as often as people in Britain and France, and half as much again as Americans. It is in the countryside that the main increase in film watching has taken place. In 1950 town dwellers went four times as often as country people, and in 1960 twice as often, but now the difference is only slight.

In 1971 there were 39 film studios producing between 160 and

K

200 full-length films a year (including films for television) and over a thousand shorts. Documentaries and feature films form a large proportion of the output, but films depicting sexual intercourse, violent crime and sadistic scenes are not made. The subjects for non-documentary films are taken either from literary classics or from modern scripts having a moral, educational or ideological theme or purpose.

MUSIC

The love of music and the ability to play musical instruments are widely diffused throughout Russia. The accordion and the balalaika are especially popular, and form the normal accompaniment to folk songs and dances. Those who are gifted receive special training in music schools and eventually find employment in the orchestras attached to restaurants, hotels and other state enterprises. For the especially talented there are the 20 conservatoires. All large towns have philharmonic orchestras which give frequent concerts, attendance at which is drawn from all classes. Besides the orchestras there are numerous choirs, chamber music groups and song and dance ensembles. Musicians are organised in the Union of Composers and are honoured and well paid. Standards are high, for the popular addiction to music of all kinds makes for a critical and discerning public.

MUSEUMS, ART GALLERIES AND LIBRARIES

Russia is a land of museums, there being about 12,000, most of them thronged not only by curious individuals but by conducted parties of schoolchildren, trade unionists and tourists. There are about 140 art galleries, the most famous being the Hermitage in Leningrad and the Tretyakov Gallery in Moscow. The Russian monarchy and aristocracy invested much of their wealth in the acquisition of fine pictures by great masters, and the Leningrad Hermitage houses a unique collection of valuable paintings from all the major European schools. In addition the Hermitage holds the largest collection of cameos and gems in the world, a unique collection of Graeco-Scythian cultural treasures, and much else of exceptional interest and value. The Tretyakov Gallery in Moscow is devoted to Russian art. Besides paintings it displays early ikons and other treasures. At the opposite end of the scale of grandeur is the humble collective farm art gallery, where all the works are likely to be by modern Soviet painters.

The Soviet Union possesses 350,000 libraries with a total of over 12½ billion books between them. About 130,000 of the libraries serve the general public, the rest being educational, scientific, technical and specialist. Some of the general libraries are located in housing blocks and there are trade union libraries at the factories. Young Russians appear passionate for reading, possibly because theirs is the first fully literate generation. Foreign books, available in translation, are in great demand. Shakespeare, Dickens, Byron, Goldsmith, Burns, Oscar Wilde, Conan Doyle, A. J. Cronin and Priestley have long been popular, but most readers now prefer more modern books such as those by John Braine, John Osborne, Joyce Carey and Doris Lessing. There are no library charges for readers or borrowers.

In 1969 Soviet publishing houses brought out 74,611 new books and pamphlets. Sixty Soviet languages and forty-one foreign languages were represented in this number, and the USSR claims to translate more foreign books than any other country. In the United States, the only comparable country, the number of new publications was 62,083 and in the UK, 32,321.

THE CIRCUS

The circus in Russia has not only maintained every whit of its popularity, but has also come to be regarded as a form of high art. The variety of its acts and the range of its equipment are beyond compare. There are fifty permanent circus halls, more than in all the other countries of the world combined, yet many more are planned. Over 45 million spectators a year watch the circus in the Soviet Union. A modern development has been the perfection of the ice circus, in which circus turns on ice are combined with figure skating; it has been described as a 'synthesis of the circus and the ice ballet'. One of the popular acts is the playing of ice hockey by teams of bears. When Russian circuses perform abroad they attract audiences which include many people who do not normally attend circuses.

PRESS, RADIO AND TELEVISION

There are very many newspapers published in the USSR at a variety of centres and in all the various languages, but the universal dailies are *Pravda* and *Izvestya*. In the Russian Republic *Sovetskaya Soyuz* is also widely read. Specialist magazines cover almost every single activity, but there are several of general interest, eg *Ogonyok*, a pictorial weekly, and the satirical *Krokodil*, which appears every ten days. The content of newspapers and magazines is closely watched by the authorities, and any departure from the guide lines set by the Party is either eliminated by the censors or, should it get past them, attacked in retrospect. Criticism in detail, however, of irregularities in administration is encouraged, and many letters and articles expose some deficiency or other, provided the blame can be laid at the door of delinquent individuals and not at that of the higher organs of Party and state. Only the Communist newspapers of foreign countries are on sale in the Soviet Union. The absence of commercial advertising or of sensationalism, sex and violence, and a generally restrained and conservative layout distinguish Soviet newspapers and magazines sharply from their Western counterparts.

There are numerous children's newspapers and magazines, the chief of which is the *Pioneerskaya Pravda*, published thrice weekly for members of the Young Pioneers. Younger children enrolled as Octoberites, have their own weekly, *Murzilka*, and there are picture papers for infants.

The distinguishing features of Soviet radio and television programmes are the considerable amount of time devoted to ideological, political and social matters and the total exclusion of triviality, pornography and violence. About 60 per cent of households in the USSR have television sets, but the vast extent of the country, which includes many sparsely peopled areas, makes eventual viewing by the whole population unlikely in the near future. Even if the technical problems were solved there remains the difficulty presented by the multiplicity of languages in the remoter areas.

Many Russians, realising that the news they receive from their own media is strictly censored and carefully selected, listen to foreign wireless stations, particularly the BBC Russian service, and the powerful *Radio Liberty* and *Voice of America* situated in West Germany. The latter two, financed from America, are more blatantly anti-Soviet than the BBC and their propaganda is probably effective in fostering discontent in Soviet Russia.

HOLIDAYS

The Soviet worker is entitled to two consecutive days off work fifty-two times a year, and these usually correspond to the weekends. In addition there are the public holidays—1 May (Labour Day) and 2 May, 7 November (Revolution Day) and 8 November, and 5 December. The minimum paid annual holiday is three weeks, but holidays are longer in remote northerly or easterly parts of the country: beyond the Arctic Circle they are six weeks. In consequence the average leisure time is much greater than formerly, and this, combined with higher wages, has made people more mobile. In 1970 the average Soviet citizen was estimated to have travelled 1,250 miles (excluding local daily journeys to work, shop, etc), over four times the estimate for 1950. Most of this travel takes place at week-ends. The average American, aided by his automobile, travels about 6,000 miles a year.

A recent official sampling survey shows that 60 million of the adult population over 16, which numbers about 170 million, took their annual holiday away from home. Of those who did so, 25 million (over 40 per cent) spent the time with relatives, with rather more going to the country than to towns. Another 18 million, or 30 per cent of those going away, spent a mobile holiday, joining organised tours or using camping sites: a large proportion of these travelled on the country's many rivers, some of them on home-made rafts. Only 10 million went to traditional beach or inland health resorts, while another 6 million (10 per cent) went to a country cottage. But in the big cities the proportion going to country cottages or *dachas* is larger—almost a quarter of the population of Leningrad spends its summer holidays in a *dacha*. By geographical area visited, most (9 million) went to the Crimea-Caucasus area, which possesses not only popular Black Sea resorts like Yalta, Sochi and Pitsunda, but inland mountain health and ski resorts. Next come the resorts of the Estonian Baltic coast such as Pjarnu and Pirita.

Sochi, on the Black Sea coast at the foot of the Caucasus Mountains, just north of the boundary between the Russian Republic and that of Georgia, is the largest Soviet holiday resort. It stretches for 19 miles along the coast and entertains over 2 million visitors a year. Yet it has only 17 hotels, and although there are also 80 trade union rest homes and sanatoria and 13 camps and camp sites, accommodation for the private visitor is difficult to find. In fact, all over the Soviet Union shortage of hotel-type accommodation is acute, and it is not surprising that the 1971–5 five-year plan contains the promise that 'more hotels, camping sites and other facilities for tourists shall be built'. It is planned to increase the capacity of tourist camps and hotels from 128,000 to 288,000.

Few Soviet citizens can experience the joys of foreign travel, but with one-sixth of the land surface of the earth at their disposal this is a small disadvantage from the purely recreational point of view. The variety of scenery, climate and open air diversion is immense: all that is wanting in many areas is an adequate provision of access and facilities, and every year brings progress in this respect. Most holidaymakers are from the more youthful age groups of the population and activity rather than rest and relaxation characterises the ways they spend their time. Hunting and fishing are favourite pastimes, both for week-ends and for the annual holiday. Winter fishing through the ice is extremely popular.

The children's summer camp is part of the life of most young people, and 8 million children a year take part in these distant out-of-door holidays which are organised by the state, by trade unions and by the Young Pioneers. One example is the *Orlyonok* (Young Eagle) camp on the Black Sea coast, which is open all the year round and takes 2,500 children aged 12–15 each month. This is not a typical holiday camp, however, for a stay at it is primarily a reward for meritorious progress in school work or at arts, crafts, hobbies or games. Those who go during the school year have lessons as well as recreation. Another example is Camp Voskhod (Sunrise) at Lake Issyk Kul (Hot Lake). The lake, which lies at 5,300ft above sea level, is surrounded by the snow-capped peaks of the Tyan Shan Mountains. It is fed by a hot spring, whence its name. A long caravan of motor coaches, preceded by a police car and escorted by police motor cycles, brings a new intake up the long, steep, tortuous and dangerous mountain road to the camp. Every summer more than 20,000 children enjoy this particular lakeside holiday. Vouchers entitling attendance at such a camp are issued free by trade unions to the children whose parents have low wages or large families, and at between one-fifth and one-third of the cost to the rest.

9

Hints for Visitors

TRAVEL TO RUSSIA

THE Soviet travel agency Intourist is responsible for all foreign travel to the USSR. The intending visitor may book his trip with them or with a local agent, preferably one who specialises in travel to Russia and the East European countries. His mode of travel and his itinerary will have to be planned beforehand and approved by Intourist, who will make all the arrangements for transport and accommodation, including meeting the traveller at airports or stations and taking him to and from his hotel. Once the arrangements have been made it will be very difficult, though not impossible, to depart from them after the journey has begun. Intourist will provide the traveller through his agent with vouchers for travel and accommodation and, if required, for meals and sight-seeing excursions.

Besides a passport, the visitor will need a Soviet visa. This should be applied for at least a week before the start of the journey and the application must be accompanied by three photographs. Visas are issued by Soviet consular offices, from which they may be obtained in person, free of charge, but most travel agencies make a charge for getting them. The traveller will only be able to stay in the places named on the visa. If he lives in a European country he will not need a vaccination certificate nor any other medical document, unless there has recently been an outbreak of smallpox, etc in his own country. If he comes from any other continent he will need a vaccination certificate.

Visitors from Britain can travel to Russia by air, rail, road and sea, those from North America by air and sea. Direct flights to Moscow are available from London, New York, Montreal and Toronto. The train journey from London, via a sea crossing from Harwich to Hook of Holland or Dover to Ostend, passes through Holland or Belgium, West Germany, East Germany and Poland and through Berlin and Warsaw. From Hook of Holland or Ostend one travels in a Russian through carriage and in a sleeper compartment with single or double berths (first class) or three berths (second class). The rail journey, which takes two and a half days, is full of interest, enabling the traveller to have a good look at the countryside, and to meet and get to know some of his fellow passengers. When the train enters the Soviet Union at Brest the carriages are lifted off their bogies by powerful hydraulic jacks; the bogies are then replaced by others of the wider Russian gauge, and the carriages are lowered down on these. The interruptions for passport and visa inspection can be irritating, especially while crossing Germany, where there are border controls entering East Germany, entering West Berlin, re-entering East Germany and leaving East Germany for Poland. Travellers by this route need Polish and East German transit visas. The East German visa is obtained on the train but the Polish visa must be obtained beforehand, and passport photographs have to accompany the application.

One can take a car to the Soviet Union and enter the country from Scandinavia, from northern Europe by way of Germany and Poland, from Central Europe by way of Austria and Hungary, and from southern Europe by way of Yugoslavia and Rumania. Transit visas will be needed for travel through most of these countries.

The journey by sea is available only in summer. Passenger vessels of the Soviet line Morflot sail from London and Montreal from May till October. Every type of accommodation is available, from the most luxurious to the spartan, although the latter is very inexpensive. These ships usually call at non-Russian Baltic seaports, eg Copenhagen and Helsinki, and remain long enough for passengers to spend several hours on shore at each. They thus offer a most interesting way of reaching Russia if one has the time. From London to Leningrad the voyage takes five days and from Montreal to Leningrad fourteen days. The Soviet Union may also be reached via the Black Sea from the Mediterranean ports of Marseilles, Genoa, Naples, Venice and Piraeus, or by an enchanting cruise down the Danube from Passau in East Germany, passing through such beautiful and historic capital cities as Vienna, Budapest and Belgrade. Passengers in the Far East can arrive at the Russian Pacific port of Nakhodka, near Vladivostok, from Yokohama or Hong Kong. If one travels by sea, a car can be transported to most Soviet ports of entry.

ENTERING THE SOVIET UNION

Before entering the country visitors must fill in a declaration about the nature of goods they are bringing with them, and the declaration, after inspection, should be retained until after leaving. The ordinary tourist seldom has his luggage or baggage examined. Reasonable quantities of any articles intended for personal use are admitted duty free, including tobacco, alcoholic liquor, perfume, cameras, etc, and if the traveller's cases are inspected the officer will probably be looking to see whether he is bringing in any anti-Soviet printed matter or goods for sale. It is illegal for a visitor to sell goods privately. Any fruit and vegetables must be offered for inspection.

Motorists have to sign a declaration that they will re-export their cars, and they must have an international driving licence and a car registration certificate or log book, but they do not need any of the other documents usually required on crossing a European frontier.

It is important to ensure that the necessary currency declaration is made, submitted and stamped on entry, as this will be required on leaving. All such forms are available in an English language version. Any amount of foreign currency may be brought in, whether in travellers' cheques or notes/bills, provided it is declared. The foreign money can be exchanged for Russian money at the point of entry. It is illegal to exchange money with any person or persons other than through an authorised state bank or agency, and the tourist should resist any private offer of a more favourable rate of exchange. It is advisable to keep the certificates given when money is exchanged, as on presentation of these any surplus Russian money one has at the end of the journey can be changed back. It is illegal to take Russian money into or out of the USSR.

ACCOMMODATION

Even if the visitor is travelling privately, and not as a member of a group, Intourist will see that he is met on arrival with a taxi which will take him to his hotel. He will not know for certain to which hotel he has been assigned until he arrives. Once in the hotel he will go to the service bureau or administrative office where he will be assigned his room, which is likely to be spacious, clean and comfortable. There are four classes of accommodation: de-luxe suite, de-luxe, first and tourist. Single- and twin-bed rooms are available in all classes. Prices vary according to season, the three seasons being 'high season' (1 July to 31 August), 'season' (25 April to 30 June and 1 September to 30 September) and 'off season' (1 October to 24 April), but the high-season rate applies only to the cities of Moscow, Leningrad and Kiev, and tourist accommodation is not then available in those towns. Elsewhere the 'season' rate applies throughout the summer. Current rates are obtainable from any Intourist office or good travel agency. In 1972 prices per person per night (bed and breakfast) ranged from 107 roubles for a single room in the 'de-luxe suite' class in the high season to 8 roubles for a twin-bed room in the tourist class in the off season. It should be pointed out that the 'de-luxe suite' class price includes a chauffeur-driven car with guide-interpreter available within the city limits from eight o'clock in the morning to midnight, while the 'de-luxe' class provides a car for three hours a day. Free conducted sight-seeing excursions are included in the price of the first and tourist classes. These prices are fixed and admit of no reduction if the cars or excursions are not taken up. All rooms have baths and showers except in the tourist class.

Those travelling by car pay lower rates because transport is not included in the price of their room. There are then only two classes, first and tourist, but tourist accommodation is not available in Moscow, Leningrad and Kiev in the high season. In some towns the motorist may be allocated to a motel instead of a hotel. In these there is only one class of room, with prices similar to those of the tourist class of a hotel. In 1972 a motorist occupying a first-class single room in a hotel in the high season would pay 19 roubles for bed and breakfast, and for a twin-bed room in the tourist class in the off season, 6 roubles. All other room prices fall between these two extremes.

Camping sites exist outside the towns and are open from 1 June to 1 September (from 15 May in the south). Camping equipment can be hired cheaply at these sites: eg a tent for two for 10 kopeks (this price, and those below, referring to 1972). Washrooms, laundry rooms, post office, telegraph and telephone and car-washing facilities are also available. Visitors to camp sites pay 50 kopeks for parking space per day and 80 kopeks for tent site, including use of shower, cooking facilities, water, sanitation and use of laundry. At some camping sites there are two-bedded bungalows where the daily rate is 3 roubles per person plus 50 kopeks for parking. The usual equipment and services are available.

FOOD

At the time of booking the traveller may elect to pay the full board rate for his accommodation. He will then be given vouchers for all meals which he can use in the hotel dining-room. Here he may have to wait a long time to be served as, in the high season, dining-rooms are overcrowded. This is mainly because they are normally open to the public as well as to hotel guests, and the waiters become overworked. Very occasionally one may even sit for an hour or two and fail to get any attention! At less busy times service is usually punctual, efficient and courteous. Tipping is a problem: it is officially frowned on, and although most waiters accept tips, many do so ungraciously and some will take offence. Yet if a visitor does not tip and the waiter happens to expect one (and some do indeed expect them, especially from foreigners) he may not be made so welcome at the next meal. Waiters may contrive their own tip by exaggerating the bill somewhat, in which case it is probably tactful not to question the addition, unless the excess is exorbitant. One solution is to order a meal that comes to slightly less than the value of the meal voucher and let the waiter keep the change, as he probably will anyway.

Meals in the hotel dining-room are usually well worth waiting for, but if one does not like waiting or wishes to save money, one should find the hotel buffet. Here service is cafeteria-style and fast. The food is inexpensive and one will probably have only Russians for company. But it is pointless to do this if one has prepaid vouchers for full meals in a dining-room as these cannot be changed back into cash. The more venturesome traveller can try shopping for food and make up his own snack. If one prepays for full board (luncheon, tea and dinner) it costs 4 roubles a day more than booking for bed and breakfast only.

TRAVEL INSIDE THE USSR

Most visitors travel from place to place in the USSR by plane and there is modern, fast and frequent service by *Aeroflot* between all major centres and many minor ones. Fares are comparable to first-class rail. Rail travel is more interesting for those who wish to see the countryside and study the people, but because many places are far apart, journeys have often to be made on long-distance trains made up entirely of sleepers. Such trains have dining cars and most of the rest have buffet cars. Arrangements for travel from town to town by air or rail have to be made beforehand at the service bureau of the traveller's hotel.

Travel by motor vehicle is possible on certain roads only, all of them in the western part of the country. They are principally: the roads from Moscow to Leningrad and Tallinn; Moscow to

Brest on the Polish border via Minsk; Moscow to Shaginia, Chop and Purobnoe on the Polish, Hungarian and Rumanian borders respectively or to Odessa via Kiev; Moscow to the Crimea via Kharkov; Moscow to the Caucasus and the Turkish border via Kharkov, Tbilisi and Yerevan; Moscow to Yaroslavl and Moscow to Vladimir. One cannot therefore drive to Siberia or Soviet Central Asia. Travel may be either in the visitor's own car or in one hired from Intourist. The daily rate for a self-drive car (1972) is 6.30 roubles for a five-seater Volga or 4.50 roubles for a four-seater Moskvich, with an extra charge according to distance travelled, and with reductions for longer periods. Chauffeur-driven cars are also available at rates varying from 22–49.50 roubles a day with extra charge according to mileage. Hired cars are available in Moscow, Sochi, Yalta, Brest, Minsk, Kiev, Kharkov, Odessa, Lvov, Tiblisi, Sukhumi, Kishinev and Yerevan. Coaches also may be hired for larger groups. Travellers by car have to be very provident with regard to petrol/gasoline and oil as petrol/gas stations are few and far between, both in the towns and along the main roads. One may have to go 200 miles before reaching the next. Prices for petrol vary from 70 kopeks for 10 litres (2·2 gallons) of 72 octane to 95 kopeks for 10 litres of 95 octane or above. It is also wise to bring all necessary tools and essential spare parts. In the Soviet Union one keeps to the right and there are the usual road signs and speed limits.

Large parts of the country, including the Urals, most of Siberia and the Far East, are closed to foreigners. Areas which foreign visitors are free to visit include Moscow and its environs; Leningrad and its environs; most of the Ukraine, including Kiev, Kharkov and Odessa; Moldavia including Kishinev; the Baltic region, including Riga and Tallinn; the Byelorussian Republic including Minsk; the Caucasus region; parts of Central Asia, including Tashkent, Bukhara, Samarkand and Khiva; and certain places along the Trans-Siberian Railway, notably Novosibirsk, Irkutsk and Khabarovsk. From Irkutsk one may travel north to the new town of Bratsk and see its hydro-electric power station, until recently the largest in the world, or southwards to Lake Baykal.

Intourist arranges tours for groups or individuals to all the above areas at very advantageous rates. Full and up-to-date details of these and all other matters pertinent to travel in the Soviet Union may be obtained from Intourist, whose London address is 292 Regent Street, W1 (telephone 01-580 4954). In New York their address is 45 East 49th Street (telephone 212-752 3030), and in Canada, 2020 Stanley Street, Montreal 110, PQ. Guide-interpreters are provided for all visitors, but one is quite free to move about on one's own within the areas listed on one's visa and detailed in one's Intourist itinerary.

PHOTOGRAPHY

According to Intourist, 'No restrictions are placed upon tourists in this respect except the usual ones you will find in any country [military objects, etc].' But when it is spelled out in detail the prohibited list includes, besides 'all military objects and institutions':

railway and highway bridges, hydrotechnical installations, sluices, dams, pumping stations, railway junctions, tunnels, industrial establishments, scientific research institutions, design offices, laboratories, electric power stations, radio beacons, radio stations, telephone and telegraph stations.

Photographs of factories, farms, mines and other industrial establishments may only be taken with the permission of the management. In practice one may easily find oneself the centre of a hostile group of angry people, one of whom will probably call the police, if one ventures to photograph anything of an industrial or commercial nature—factories, bridges, railways, and even a garage or petrol station or a public market. The policeman's reaction may be anything from a smiling warning to be careful, once the irate objectors have dispersed, to the removal of the film from the camera. The experience of the war, survival in which was due in part to the tightest security precautions, and the distrust of foreigners inculcated at various times by government propaganda, have made Soviet citizens extremely suspicious of the activities of foreigners from capitalist countries, and although those in groups, shepherded by Russian guides, are considered harmless, the individual travelling on his own with a camera is at greater risk of having his intentions misunderstood. Photography from aircraft or within 25 kilometres of the frontier is strictly forbidden.

Many individuals in Russia resent also being photographed without their consent having been previously asked and granted. The traveller who exercises tact, discretion and caution is not likely to be seriously impeded in photographing objects of interest. Although film and developing facilities are available it is advisable to bring film to which one is accustomed.

CLIMATE AND CLOTHING

The winter is severe and snowy in most parts of the country, so that plenty of warm clothing and a pair of good boots are recommended for winter travel. Summer, on the other hand, can be quite hot, and the southern parts of the country very hot, so that the summer visitor needs only light clothing; a light raincoat is also advisable, as frequent short sharp showers occur. Spring is the season of the thaw, with mud, slush and water everywhere away from the main streets. Good waterproof boots are essential if the traveller intends venturing about on his own. Cold wintry weather may reappear during this season in the central and northern parts of the country, making warm clothing again necessary. Autumn can be a showery season with cold nights and warm days and the visitor should be prepared accordingly.

SIGHT-SEEING AND ENTERTAINMENT

Sight-seeing excursions and visits to museums, art galleries, exhibitions, the theatre, the ballet, the circus and even the cinema are best arranged through the service bureau of the visitor's hotel where the clerks speak several foreign languages, including English. There are always a variety of conducted sight-seeing tours or other excursions on offer, and most visitors will be entitled to sample at least one of these free of charge, according to the prepaid vouchers they hold. The streets of all Russian towns, even the largest, become quiet after ten o'clock at night and, in the absence of neon signs and shop window lighting, they are then relatively dark, with only the street lamps and traffic lights visible. There are no public houses in the English sense, no bars and no night clubs.

MEDICAL AID

Medical services are readily available without charge and if a traveller becomes ill he should seek aid through his hotel's service bureau or his guide-interpreter. He may have to pay for drugs if his illness should prove lengthy.

POSTS AND TELECOMMUNICATIONS

All the usual communication services are available in the USSR and, for the traveller whose knowledge of Russian is not adequate for use in the ordinary post office or telephone kiosk, service is available in his Intourist hotel from English-speaking clerks.

TIME

Moscow time is always two hours ahead of Greenwich Mean Time and one hour ahead of British Summer Time. Moscow time is used throughout the country in timetables, but for local use the country is divided into eleven time zones.

L

TRANSIT THROUGH THE USSR

Because the journey is shorter, quicker and more interesting, it is becoming more popular to travel from Europe to the Far East and to India and Pakistan by way of the Soviet Union, often including a short stop at a Soviet town or towns. Arrangements are made by Intourist for travel from London to Yokohama or Hong Kong by the trans-Siberian route with various combinations of air, rail and sea travel for prices between £134 and £270 per person, according to mode and class of travel, including meals onward from Moscow. Soviet transit visas are needed for such travel. Several foreign airlines also now use the trans-Siberian route.

MEETING RUSSIANS

The Russians are a very informal and uninhibited people in social intercourse, and a handshake, hug or even a kiss may be given on meeting and leaving, according to the degree of warmth felt. The universal greeting is *zdravstvuite* ('your good health'), and on parting *do svidaniya* ('until we meet again') or *do skorovo svidaniya* ('may we soon meet again'). 'Please' is *pozhaluista,* and 'thank you' *spasibo.* A useful word is *mozhno?* used with an interrogative tone. This means 'Is it possible?' or 'Is it allowed?' It can be used in restaurants to ask if a seat is free or in asking permission to do this, that or the other, for instance, before taking photographs. As the answer can be readily given by a nod or shake of the head, it can be used effectively by the non-Russian speaker. The verbal affirmative answer to *mozhno?* is *mozhno* (possible). 'No' is *nyet* (the 'y' pronounced as in the English word 'yet'), and 'yes' *da.*

Russians are very hospitable and expect their guests to consume large quantities of food and drink, and any visitor to a Russian home should make ready for this by as long a period of abstinence beforehand as he can manage. They are also generous with presents, and even a chance meeting with a foreign stranger on the street is likely to end with some little gift being pressed into his hand. Visitors should therefore carry a small assortment of gifts which can be given in return, or used to show appreciation of some service. They are more acceptable than tips to all but the most mercenary. Chocolates, English cigarettes, handkerchiefs, pens and pencils may be given, and for those able to read them, especially guide-interpreters who are likely to be students of English, books in that language.

Since the Revolution Russians have used the word *tovarishch* when addressing each other, and this word is also used before names as an equivalent of 'Mr'. But when they are addressing foreigners from capitalist countries, *gospodin* ('gentleman') is used instead. Officials, when speaking to Russians, employ the form of address *grazhdanin* (masculine) or *grazhdanka* (feminine), meaning 'citizen'.

Acknowledgements

THE author is indebted to his wife, Marjorie, and to his son, William, for much valuable help. He also wishes to acknowledge the aid, generously and willingly given as always, of Mr P. C. Masters of the School of Geography at Oxford.

The quotations in the text are derived as follows:

page 23: John Carr. *A Northern Summer* (London, 1804)

pages 23–4: Richard Chancellor in *The Principall Navigations, Voiages and Discoveries of the English Nation*, Richard Hakluyt (London, 1589)

page 25: Dimitri Obolensky. 'Russia's Byzantine Heritage', *Oxford Slavonic Papers*, vol I

page 42: L. G. Churchward. *Contemporary Soviet Government* (New York, 1968)

page 56: Nevill Forbes in *Russia from the Varangians to the Bolsheviks*, R. Beazley and others (Oxford, 1918)

Index